BATTLES IN FOCUS
CASSINO

IAN GOODERSON

BRASSEY'S

Left: Monte Cassino, showing the shell-torn trees and debris before it.

This book is dedicated in fond memory to Ronald Arthur Oxford (1921–1984), a close friend to my family and who, when I was young, first told me of Monte Cassino, for when he was young he had been a British soldier of the Italian Campaign

Copyright © Ian Gooderson, 2003
All rights reserved. No part of this publication may be reproduced, stored in a retrieval system or transmitted in any form or by any means; electronic, electrostatic, magnetic tape, mechanical, photocopying, recording or otherwise, without permission in writing from the publishers.

First published in 2003 by Brassey's

A member of Chrysalis Books plc

Brassey's
The Chrysalis Building, Bramley Road,
London W10 6SP

North American orders:
Casemate Publishing, 2114 Darby Road,
Havertown, PA 19083, USA

Ian Gooderson has asserted his moral right to be identified as the author of this work.

Library of Congress Cataloging in Publication Data available

British Library cataloguing in Publication Data
A catalogue record for this book is available from the British Library

ISBN 1 85753 324 0

All photographs: Chrysalis Images
Cover illustration courtesy New Zealand National Archives

Edited and designed by DAG Publications Ltd
Designed by David Gibbons
Edited by Michael Boxall
Cartography by Anthony A. Evans

Printed in Spain.

Author's Note
The author wishes to state that the views expressed in this book are his own and not necessarily those of the Joint Services Command and Staff College, the Ministry of Defence, or of any other agency of the British Government.

CONTENTS

Introduction, 6

1 THE STRATEGIC IMPERATIVES, 9
Italy, 1943

2 THROUGH THE BERNHARDT LINE, 20

3 THE TIME IMPERATIVE, 37
Fifth Army and 'Shingle'

4 THE FIRST BATTLE OF CASSINO, 44

5 THE SECOND AND THIRD BATTLES OF CASSINO, 75

6 MONTE CASSINO: A POLISH BATTLE, 99

7 CASSINO AND CONTROVERSY, 116

Notes, 121

Index, 128

INTRODUCTION

The lessons and experience they have gained should be of value to those who follow them, in this Theater and elsewhere.

General Mark W. Clark, 1944[1]

The mist-shrouded slopes of Monte Cassino were uncannily quiet on the morning of 18 May 1944. Then, shortly before 10 o'clock, soldiers wearing the battle-dress and distinctive dish-shaped steel helmets of the British army heard a bugle playing from within the bomb- and shell-blasted ruins of the monastery that still towered above them. Few of the combat-hardened soldiers who heard it were unmoved, for it was sounding their country's traditional military call, the *Hejnal*. A rudimentary flag, improvised from parts of a Red Cross emblem and a blue handkerchief, flew from the ruins. It was the pennant of the 12th Podolski Lancers, the Reconnaissance Regiment of the 3rd Carpathian Rifle Division, which had ordered a patrol to investigate the suspiciously quiet monastery. The thirteen Lancers had cautiously entered the ruins to find its German paratroop defenders gone, leaving only a handful of their wounded behind.[2] Monte Cassino, that had defied capture by the Allied armies in Italy for five months, was in the hands of the British Eighth Army's II Polish Corps.

The *Hejnal* that morning signalled the end of not one, but in fact four major battles fought in the Cassino area between January and May 1944 that are the subject of this book. These battles saw some of the hardest fighting of the Italian Campaign, indeed of the Second World War, but that alone would be insufficient justification for adding further to their already extensive historiography. The strategic background to the Italian Campaign and the course of events that led the Allied and German armies to confront one other at Cassino, already well recorded by historians,[3] will only be lightly touched upon here. The course of the Cassino battles has also received detailed attention, and this book will not repeat the furrow so ably ploughed.[4]

This book is a study in battle reconstruction. Its purpose is to recreate the circumstances, opportunities and decisions of battle; to reproduce the imperatives that drove the combatants and the pressures under which they fought. While predominantly a work of military history, the purpose of this reconstruction is also to establish the relevance of historical experience. The Cassino battles belong to the past; their weapons and methods obsolete. Battles, however, are human activities, and the ever-present human factor in war has a more than historical relevance. To understand a battle, the reasons why opposing commanders behaved as they did and the methods employed by their armies, requires an appreciation of their perceptions then. The fate of soldiers and the outcome of battles reflect decisions and actions based upon an interpretation of that which was known, or believed to be known, at the time. Of all the weapons of war, information and its skilful employment or manipulation has proven one of the most decisive; it was certainly decisive in Italy in the spring of 1944. Battles also generate their own dynamics, their own momentum, and once launched they can rapidly pass beyond the control of those who initiated them. For the Allies trying to reach Rome in 1944, this was one of their most painful lessons. Information, leadership, and the dynamics of battle are critical factors in warfare. They will remain so despite its rapidly changing nature, and historical experience is the most valuable of signposts guiding our evaluation of them.

From a historical perspective, the Cassino battles are the Italian Campaign in microcosm. In a battle area comparatively compressed in space and time, these battles involved mountain warfare, river crossing operations, and urban fighting in the town of Cassino itself. They also involved, with very mixed success, the use of armour, and with equally mixed success attempts to influence the course of the ground fighting by the employment of air power. In the Cassino battles, the opposing armies and their weapons and tactics confronted the variations of the Italian terrain, and for much of the fighting, they confronted them during a severe winter. Considered from the German perspective, the Cassino battles are a model of defensive warfare, revealing maximum effective exploitation of terrain and firepower combined with the stubborn fighting qualities of highly proficient and well-motivated troops. Viewed from the Allied perspective, these battles are a study in the problems of attack. They indicate the extent to which progress and momentum ultimately depend upon the determination and endurance of the attackers, and the extent to which firepower and tactical innovation can assist them. In battle, attacks can falter and break down because of a combination of factors; the Cassino battles reveal them all. For the Allies, these were also coalition battles, and the consequent tensions and the insights they provide into coalition warfare have a resonance beyond the historical context of 1944.

Each of the Cassino battles reconstructed for this study is set in its strategic context, with the imperatives influencing the decisions of both the Allied and German commanders. The planning and conduct of the battles is examined from the operational level, but where appropriate the focus narrows to the tactical to highlight decisive periods in the fighting, and significant examples of tactics' and weapons' effectiveness. The reader progresses chronologically but also analytically step by step through the decision making and the combats, assimilating an awareness of the limitations of information and the pressure of time, the combination that has always constituted battle, and always will.

There is something further to add to this introduction to a study of the Cassino battles. Military historians, like soldiers, are unaccustomed to battles of allegorical significance. They rarely confront a challenge such as that laid down, perhaps unwittingly, by Saint Benedict in the sixth century when he founded his monastery on the crest of that 1,700-foot hill overlooking the Roman town that

INTRODUCTION

became Cassino. The challenge is not only to describe and analyse the military operations involved but to convey the distinctive atmosphere in which they took place. For Saint Benedict, in choosing the site of what had been a Roman temple to Apollo, did more than symbolise the triumph of Christianity. In seeking security for his monastery, he chose defender's ground of great strategic significance, dominating the Roman *via Casilina*, known to later generations as Highway 6, one of the principal roads leading to Rome. He thereby ensured that at Cassino two conflicting elements in the nature of humanity, religious faith and the pursuit of God, and war, the pursuit of destruction, would confront each other face to face. The consciousness of this among soldiers enduring the stress of battle, the bitterness, the heightened sense of irony, the sharpened moral dilemma, the introspection, are the backcloth to the battles of Cassino. Like the monastery, either intact or in its gaunt ruins, it is always there; few battles have affected the minds of men in quite the same way as those fought at Cassino in 1944.

THE STRATEGIC IMPERATIVES
ITALY, 1943

On 2 October 1943 the British and American Allies received the first of several indications of a significant change in German strategy in Italy. Through 'Ultra', the interception and decryption of German 'Enigma' signals traffic, they obtained a report of an interview between Hitler and the commander of German forces in southern Italy, Field Marshal Albert Kesselring. Hitler ordered an active defence along the entire front of the Tenth Army facing the Allies, and the relinquishing of as little ground as possible.[1] Several days later, further decrypts became available, this time of signals from German Air Force (*Luftwaffe*) liaison officers with LXXVI Panzer Corps, holding Tenth Army's left flank against General Bernard Montgomery's British Eighth Army. These signals clarified the boundaries between the LXXVI Panzer Corps and Tenth Army's right flank formation, the XIV Panzer Corps fighting against General Mark Clark's United States Fifth Army. They also referred to a winter defensive line, the Bernhardt Line, later known to the Allies as the Winter Line. The Allies now knew without doubt that the German intention was to defend Italy along a line south of Rome.[2]

This knowledge was a serious blow to Allied hopes for their campaign on the Italian mainland which had begun on 3 September, when Montgomery's Eighth Army had crossed the Straits of Messina from Sicily and landed in Calabria. Six days later, on 9 September, Clark's US Fifth Army had landed in the Gulf of Salerno, to the south of Naples. Whereas Eighth Army confronted stubborn and delaying rearguard actions as units of LXXVI Panzer Corps retreated northwards, at Salerno Clark's Anglo-American landing force came ashore to face a desperate eight-day battle. In line with Kesselring's directives, the commander of Tenth Army, General Heinrich von Vietinghoff, concentrated elements of several divisions against the beachhead, and came close to destroying it. Despite the courage of the Allied soldiers, were it not for their heavy naval gunfire support and the weight of air power thrown into the battle, Vietinghoff would very likely have succeeded. At the cost of 3,472 casualties, the Germans inflicted 8,659 on Clark's force,[3] and they had given the Allied commanders a sobering insight into the phenomenal reaction capability of the German army that they would not soon forget. After breaking off the battle at Salerno, Vietinghoff conformed to Kesselring's instructions to withdraw gradually northwards in stages, following a 'scorched earth' policy of destroying anything of value. The pursuing Allied armies of General Sir Harold Alexander's Fifteenth Army Group, Eighth Army on the Adriatic side of the Italian peninsula and US Fifth Army on the western seaboard, discovered how the mountainous terrain, intersected by rivers, favoured the defender. There were few roads suitable for mechanised armies, and demolitions, roadblocks and skilfully laid minefields repeatedly delayed the progress of their forward units. It was a terrain in which comparatively small

THE STRATEGIC IMPERATIVES

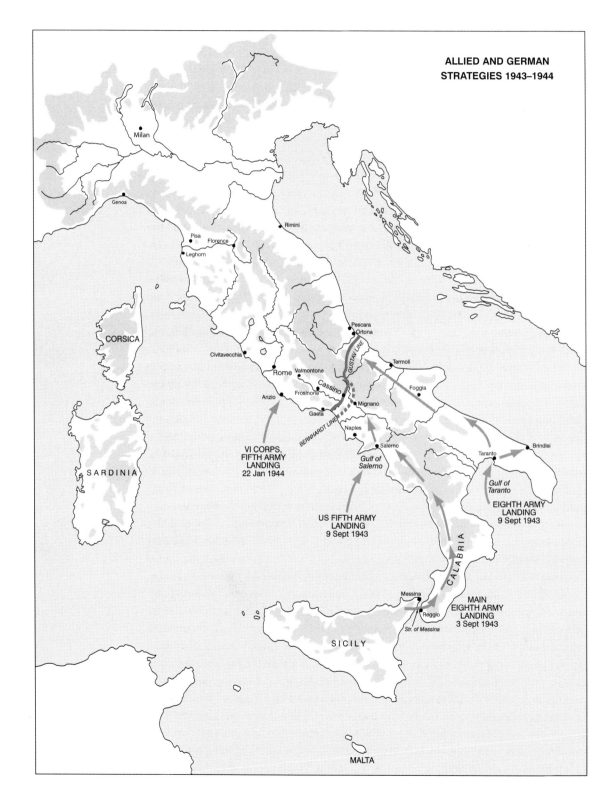

forces of determined troops supported by a few tanks and well-sited guns and mortars could hold off for hours, perhaps days, several times their own number. It was poor tank country, offering little scope for the deployment of armour in strength. Yet, despite the frustrations of maintaining an advance in such circumstances, there remained considerable Allied optimism. In withdrawing northwards, the Germans were conforming to the expectation prevalent when earlier in the year, British Prime Minister Winston Churchill and his Chiefs of Staff had succeeded in overcoming an American reluctance to commit forces to an Italian campaign.

At the 'Trident' Conference in Washington in May between Churchill and President Franklin Roosevelt and their Joint Chiefs of Staff, the Americans had firmly relegated the Mediterranean to a secondary theatre. 'Trident' asserted the primacy of operation 'Overlord', the cross-Channel invasion to begin the liberation of Western Europe in 1944, for which detailed planning and the concentration of forces was to commence. These would include seven veteran Allied divisions scheduled to leave the Mediterranean theatre in late 1943, and the removal from theatre of most of the assault shipping and landing-craft. For the first time, at 'Trident' the Allies produced a detailed inventory of their forces available to meet their global war commitments against Germany and Italy in Europe and Japan in the Far East and Pacific. The resulting document, completed in a prodigious 48-hour feat of staff work, outlined that following the projected invasion of Sicily, scheduled for July, and excluding those divisions to be withdrawn, there would be twenty-seven Allied divisions available for the Mediterranean.[4] Beyond this, the Americans would not go for fear of compromising 'Overlord', but these divisions represented a significant force, though the necessary withdrawal of assault shipping would inevitably restrict its offensive capability.

Churchill believed passionately that the Mediterranean theatre offered great potential for operations to weaken and shatter the increasingly fragile German-Italian Axis. The Americans, however, considered it a sideshow, and a potentially dangerous diversion from the main line of attack against Germany. The outcome of 'Trident' was a great personal disappointment to Churchill, but he still argued a strong case for further Mediterranean operations following a successful invasion of Sicily. A blow directed against Italy, whose loyalty to Germany increasingly wavered and where support for Benito Mussolini's Fascist dictatorship was in decline, might remove her from the war. This would support both 'Overlord' and ease the pressure upon Britain and America's hard-pressed ally in the east, Russia. It would compel Hitler to divert significant forces from occupied western Europe and from his Eastern Front to protect his southern flank in Italy and the Balkans, where the Italian garrisons would have to be replaced by German troops. Despite Churchill's eloquence and the force of his argument, the most he achieved was a directive from the Allied Combined Chiefs of Staff to General Dwight Eisenhower, the Allied Commander-in-Chief in the Mediterranean. Eisenhower was to plan operations to follow-up the invasion of Sicily 'best calculated to eliminate Italy from the war and contain the maximum number of German forces', with the final decision reserved to the Combined Chiefs.[5]

Immediately following 'Trident' Churchill, accompanied by General Sir Alan Brooke, the Chief of the Imperial General Staff, and a sceptical General George Marshall, the US Army Chief of Staff, visited Eisenhower's Allied Force Headquarters in Algiers. In the ensuing discussions Eisenhower and his Anglo-American staff, including his deputy the British General Sir Harold Alexander, were of the opinion that landings upon the Italian mainland should follow quickly upon a successful conclusion of the Sicily invasion. This would be a far more damaging blow against Italy than the alternative possibilities of seizing the islands of Corsica and Sardinia.[6] At this stage, there was considerable confidence that if Italy collapsed the Germans would be unable to find sufficient forces to garrison the country, and that they would have to withdraw to the north. In April, the British Joint Intelligence Committee concluded that with the resulting additional commitments in the Balkans and southern France the Germans would be unable to hold a defensive line in Italy even as far south as Ravenna to Pisa.[7] At the Algiers meeting, Churchill was the enthusiastic driving force, telling Eisenhower that he would celebrate Christmas 1943 with him in Rome.

There was little to cast doubt upon this optimism during the ensuing weeks between the end of May and the beginning of September. The Allied invasion of Sicily, launched on 10 July, resulted in some hard and costly fighting against stubborn German resistance, but by 17 August the island was secure. Italian resistance had largely melted away after the first few days of the invasion, and in Italy on 25 July came the fall of Mussolini. Following a vote of no confidence in the Fascist Grand Council, the King of Italy, Victor Emmanuel, had him arrested and appointed a military government under Marshal Pietro Badoglio. By this time, the Allied Combined Chiefs had provisionally accepted plans for landings on the Italian mainland within fighter cover range, formally recommended by Eisenhower and his staff. These involved landings across the Straits of Messina by Montgomery's Eighth Army, Operation 'Baytown', and a landing in the Gulf of Salerno near Naples by Clark's Fifth Army to seize the port and advance northwards on Rome, Operation 'Avalanche'. Churchill had been a strong advocate of the 'Avalanche' concept. He saw no reason why the Allied armies landed in Italy 'should crawl up the leg like a harvest bug from the ankle' when their superiority at sea and in the air enabled them to strike directly at the knee. On 26 July, the day after Mussolini's arrest, the Combined Chiefs instructed Eisenhower to plan to mount 'Avalanche' as soon as possible.

Badoglio's first move was to affirm loyalty to the Axis and the continuation of the war, a ploy intended to forestall immediate German military reaction because soon afterwards the Allies received Italian peace-feelers. Few Germans were fooled, however, and certainly not Hitler, who nevertheless desisted from his initial inclination on hearing of Mussolini's fall to order German troops near Rome to seize Badoglio and his government. Instead, the Germans played the

Italians at their own game, maintaining the fiction of a united Axis, while moving earmarked divisions to the Italian border. Although Mussolini's arrest had been a surprise to Hitler, the Germans had long been aware of the possibility of Italian defection from the Axis. Since the end of May, the German Oberkommando der Wehrmacht (OKW)[8] had contingency plans in place for German troops to seize control of the Alpine passes between Italy and the Reich, and to take-over Italian-held sectors of the Balkans. During August, Italian emissaries making clandestine contact with the Allies gave some of the earliest indications that the Germans were in fact planning to reinforce their troops in Italy. On 15 August General Castellano, Chief of Staff to the Italian General Staff, made contact through the British embassy in Madrid. With Badoglio's authority, he gave assurances that if armistice terms could be agreed, Italy would fight alongside the Allies against Germany. He also reported that the Germans had thirteen divisions in Italy, with more on the way. By 20 August, interception and decryption of German signals proved him right. This confirmed that, including the remnants of four divisions evacuated from Sicily, there were sixteen German divisions in Italy or expected to arrive there, with a new Army Group B Headquarters formed to control those in the north.[9] In fact, Hitler had designated Field Marshal Erwin Rommel to command Army Group B, with orders to prepare to take over northern Italy.

Churchill and Roosevelt with their Combined Chiefs of Staff received Castellano's proposals and information while at the 'Quadrant' conference at Quebec. On 24 August they confirmed Eisenhower's plans for 'Baytown' and 'Avalanche', and the Allied objectives in Italy. These were, in the first phase, the elimination of Italy as a belligerent and the securing of air bases in the Rome area and further north if possible. The seizure of Sardinia and Corsica would follow. In the third phase, the Allied armies would maintain 'unremitting pressure' on the German forces in northern Italy to create the conditions necessary for 'Overlord' and for an invasion of southern France.[10] By now, however, there was some concern emanating from Eisenhower's Allied Force Headquarters. The fighting in Sicily had indicated the likely strength and ferocity of German reaction, indeed the thirty-eight day campaign had cost more than 20,000 Allied casualties. Moreover, despite Allied sea and air power, the Germans successfully evacuated across the Straits of Messina more than 50,000 of their troops and much of their equipment. While Montgomery's 'Baytown' landing was likely to meet little resistance, there was now anxiety that even with their existing forces in southern Italy the Germans might concentrate rapidly against Clark's 'Avalanche' landing force and overwhelm it.[11] This force would be initially vulnerable until firmly established ashore in depth and built up and maintained by sea, but the Allies decided to accept the risk, believing that their sea power and air superiority weighed the scales sufficiently in their favour.[12] Moreover, Castellano provided further, more reassuring, information that was considered reliable; in the event of an Allied invasion of Italy, the Germans intended to hold a line between Pisa and Rimini, or if that proved untenable a line even further north along the River Po.[13] Therefore the risk of some stiff fighting in southern Italy was acceptable, and an Italian campaign feasible with the comparatively limited resources available, because the Germans would ultimately follow a strategy of withdrawing well to the north of Rome.

As events unfolded, this Allied intelligence picture remained unchanged. Eisenhower received instructions to offer 'Short Terms' to Castellano for an armistice with Italy. These included simultaneous Allied and Italian announcements of an armistice at the time of the Allied landings, and the dispatch of the Italian fleet and air forces to Allied-held ports and airfields. The Allies also enjoined upon the Italians the obligation of resisting the Germans and assisting the Allies wherever possible. The Italians finally accepted these terms shortly before 'Avalanche'. A planned landing of the US 82nd Airborne Division on the Rome airports to support the Italians was aborted only just before take-off, following frantic Italian appeals that German strength was too great and that it would only provoke greater German reprisal. The Italians also appealed for the cancellation of the armistice announcement for fear of provoking a German take-over, but this Eisenhower refused. A few hours before the 'Avalanche' force landed at Salerno, he broadcast news of the armistice, followed shortly by Badoglio's own announcement. The Germans, taken initially by surprise, reacted vigorously and implemented Operation 'Achse' (Axis), their by now well-laid plans to disarm Italian forces and seize control of important military facilities and communications. They met little organised resistance; the Italian High Command, equally surprised by the timing of the announcement, had not issued precise instructions to its army commanders.[14]

On 14 September, while Clark's troops in the Salerno beachhead were still fighting to stay ashore, Kesselring instructed Tenth Army to fall back on the Rome area after completing its operations at Salerno, regardless of whether the Allies had been forced back into the sea or not.[15] This was in line with the strategy adopted by the OKW and Hitler during August, that if Italy deserted the Axis and the Allies invaded the mainland, the surest means of extricating German forces in southern Italy would be for them to withdraw steadily northwards into central Italy. Thereafter, they would move north to link up with Army Group B, and come under Rommel's command. At this stage Hitler had no thought of defending southern Italy, or of trying to hold the Allies south of Rome, though he was receiving conflicting advice on this from his two principal commanders in theatre. Rommel argued the impossibility of retaining southern and central Italy in the face of the Allies' overwhelming air and sea power that would enable them to outflank any defensive line, and advocated a defence in northern Italy. Kesselring completely disagreed, arguing that the terrain in Italy would at least allow a staged withdrawal, and that if given the necessary resources he could hold the Allies south of Rome and deny them the propaganda coup of its capture. This, he argued, would deny the Allies a staging area from which to launch an invasion of the Balkans, a particular concern of Hitler's. Kesselring, being an airman and a *Luftwaffe* officer, also had a keen appreciation of air strategy. He realised the advantage that possession of the airfields around Foggia and Naples would give to the Allies for their strategic bombing of Germany. In Allied possession, these airfields would bring industrial targets in southern Germany and Austria, and the Roumanian oilfields, hitherto unscathed, within range of systematic air attack. At the very least, these airfields in Allied hands should remain under threat of German attack, and Germany's fighter defence be accorded the maximum possible depth, both of which required holding ground to the south of Rome.[16]

Until Hitler decided between his rival commanders, he kept the German forces in Italy evenly balanced, eight divisions under Rommel in the north and eight under Kesselring in the south, the latter including two divisions near Rome. His indecision also kept the Allies optimistic about the progress of the campaign even after the close-run beachhead battle at Salerno. Kesselring proved his case by successfully delaying the Allied advance, and preparing the Bernhardt Line which he believed could be held with eleven divisions, whereas holding northern Italy along the Apennines would require some thirteen to twenty divisions. The combination of Kesselring's skilful handling of the battle in the south, his optimism in contrast to Rommel's irritating pessimism, and Hitler's desire to protect the Balkans and retain as much of Italy as possible for a puppet Fascist regime clinched Hitler's decision. Early in October he reversed the strategy of withdrawal and accepted Kesselring's concept of a defence in the south and a firm defence along the Bernhardt Line, significantly ordering Rommel for the first time to send reinforcements south to Kesselring. Learning this through their signals intelligence caused the Allies considerable dismay, and Eisenhower reported the 'drastic change within the last forty-eight hours'. Churchill, cabling Roosevelt on 10 October, acknowledged that 'we have always trusted this kind of evidence and I therefore agree that we must now look forward to very heavy fighting before Rome is reached instead of merely pushing back rearguards.'[17] In November, Hitler appointed Kesselring Commander-in-Chief Southwest and of Army Group C, his command to embrace the entire Italian theatre. Rommel eventually left Italy for France to supervise the defences along the Channel coast, his Army Group B becoming Fourteenth Army under General Eberhard von Mackensen and part of Kesselring's command. By then, the Allies knew that in Italy they confronted the prospect of a major campaign.

In an appreciation dated 24 October, General Sir Harold Alexander outlined just how difficult that campaign was likely to be. A German defence south of Rome placed his armies at a serious disadvantage. Eleven divisions in the Fifth and Eighth Armies opposed nine German divisions in the south who held the significant advantage of a terrain allowing no scope for the Allies to deploy their superiority in armour and artillery. Moreover, there were reportedly a further fifteen German divisions in the north, making a total of twenty-four. In contrast,

THE STRATEGIC IMPERATIVES

Right: The German Commander-in-Chief in Italy, Field-Marshal Kesselring (seated) and the commander of the IV Panzer Corps, General von Senger und Etterlin confer over their battle situation maps.

the build-up rate of the Allied armies was slowing down, with at most seventeen divisions likely to be in Italy by the end of January 1944. The principal cause was lack of shipping, exacerbated by the decision of the Combined Chiefs of Staff to allocate vessels to help transport the heavy bomber squadrons of the Fifteenth USAAF to the airfields captured near Foggia as part of the Combined Bomber Offensive against Germany. The approaching winter weather would curtail the effectiveness of air support for the armies, and there was no shipping to mount an amphibious outflanking operation of sufficient strength to unhinge the German defences and speed the Allied advance. Yet for all that, Alexander acknowledged that the Allies could not accept a stabilised front south of Rome. Not only did the Italian capital now have a political significance outweighing its strategic importance, it was also necessary to gain sufficient ground to ensure the security of the Foggia airfields and the port of Naples. In other words, the threat that Kesselring determined to hold over the Allies, that the Germans might amass sufficient forces to launch an offensive and threaten the vital port and airfields, had to be prevented by placing them beyond reach. Moreover, the imperative to draw German forces into Italy in order to assist 'Overlord' required offensive pressure; 'we cannot afford to adopt a purely defensive role', observed Alexander, 'for this would entail the surrender of the initiative to the Germans'. In fact, Hitler's decision to stand fast south of Rome presented the Allies, who had embarked upon a campaign in Italy with limited forces, with an awkward strategic dilemma they would never satisfactorily solve. Alexander warned that his armies were committed to a long and costly 'slugging match' to reach Rome that could leave them weakened and exhausted.[18]

> **Field Marshal Albert Kesselring,** fifty-eight years old when Hitler appointed him Commander-in-Chief of German forces in Italy in November 1943, began his military career in the artillery. By the end of the First World War, he was serving on the General Staff, but during Hitler's rearmament of Germany he transferred to the new Luftwaffe. In 1939 he commanded Luftflotte (Air Fleet) I during the invasion of Poland, and Luftflotte II during the Battle of Britain. Luftflotte II operated in support of Army Group Centre during the invasion of Russia, but in December 1941, he assumed command of the Luftwaffe in the Mediterranean theatre. In Italy, he proved a determined and resourceful commander, whose campaign was a model of defensive warfare.

That was precisely Kesselring's intention, though he was unaware of the shipping constraints preventing the Allied seaborne landing on his flank that he constantly feared and retained mobile reserves to guard against. His object was to delay the Allied advance along a series of temporary defensive lines across Italy. Holding these for as long as possible, the troops of Tenth Army would gain valuable time for him to fortify a major defensive position and, in his own words, the Allies 'would break their teeth on it'.[19] By the end of October he had already identified this position, a formidable natural barrier running across the narrowest point of the Italian peninsula. Traced from west to east this was a line following the courses inland of the rivers Garigliano, Gari and Rapido. From the upper

Rapido, it crossed the Abruzzi Mountains to Castel di Sangro and extended to the mouth of the River Sangro on the Adriatic. This was the Gustav Line and throughout the autumn German army construction units, Todt Organisation labour battalions and Italian prisoners turned it into a fortress under the direction of Pioneer General Bessel, to whom Kesselring's frequent inspections must have been, as Kesselring later acknowledged, a thorough nuisance.[20]

Kesselring was confident of where the main effort of an Allied offensive towards Rome must come, for the terrain dictated it. Along the Adriatic coast, the British Eighth Army faced a succession of mountain valleys through which, in winter, ran swollen rivers. This was not the terrain over which to stage a sustained attack, nor did the main road routes to Rome pass through this sector. It would be along the western coast of Italy, in the sector of Clark's Fifth Army that the main Allied thrust must come, for here were the two principal routes to Rome. Along the coastal strip between the Tyrrhenian Sea and the Aurunci Mountains ran Highway 7, the ancient *Via Appia*. From the German perspective, this offered the Allies the advantage of proximity to the coast and therefore of naval support, but as a main axis of advance it was unlikely. For considerable lengths, it passed through the southern Aurunci Mountains, under their steep cliffs, and it was also prone to heavy flooding from the lower Garigliano; here the deployment of mechanised units and armour would be impossible.[21] The Allies would have to come to Rome along Highway 6, the *Via Casilina*, and they would do so because of the Liri Valley.

The staff of Fifth Army concurred with this assessment. In 1943, the Liri Valley, an expanse of low ground some fifteen miles inland, offered the only route to Rome through which a mechanised army could manoeuvre. To the north and south were mountains. On the northern side, a chain of heights lead to the Apennine range, that form a spine running the length of Italy. In 1943, their steep slopes and rough surfaces rendered any cross-country movement by troops extremely difficult and, in many places, impossible.[22] With the Apennines a formidable barrier, especially in winter, there was no possibility of Eighth Army outflanking from the Adriatic sector the German defensive lines before Rome. To the south of the Liri Valley, the Aurunci Mountains defied all but infantry and pack animals. The Liri Valley, a belt of pasture, woodlands and cornfields some twenty miles in length and up to ten miles wide, through which ran Highway 6, was the gateway to Rome. Only here, observed a Fifth Army report in November 1943, was the use of large armoured units possible.[23] By the time of that report, Kesselring was preparing to block both the southern entrance and the northern exit of the Liri Valley. At the northern exit, in the rear of the Gustav Line, was the Hitler Line, a stop-line running from the north-western exit of the valley to Terracina on the coast. Barring the southern entrance to the Liri Valley was not only the Gustav Line itself but also a bastion of it set forward of the river Garigliano, the Bernhardt Line or, to the Allies, the Winter Line.[24]

It was by now apparent to the Allied commanders in Italy that the only alternative to costly and prolonged frontal attacks, and the only means of an early capture of Rome, was an amphibious flank operation. Following a meeting with his senior Mediterranean commanders at Carthage on 3 November, Eisenhower contacted the Combined Chiefs of Staff. He requested permission to retain, until 15 December, all fifty-six British and twelve of the American Landing Ships Tanks (LSTs) scheduled to leave for Britain. Three days later, he received their approval, and an amphibious landing to outflank the German defences before Rome became at least feasible. Plans for maintaining the advance on the mainland developed with this in view. On 8 November, Alexander directed Eighth Army to attack to reach the River Pescara, some 25 miles further beyond the River Sangro. It was then to move along the Pescara Valley along Highway 5 to Avezzano, some 50 miles from Rome, and threaten the capital from the east. Clark's Fifth Army would maintain its frontal drive along Highway 6, through the Liri Valley to Frosinone. At this point, it would be within sufficient supporting distance of an amphibious assault launched in the Rome area, having already penetrated the Bernhardt and Gustav defences.[25] Despite the planned reinforcement of Fifth Army by the accelerated deployment to Italy of two French divisions from North Africa, this concept was to prove hopelessly optimistic. It was the end of the year before Eighth Army cleared the Sangro, and the middle of January 1944 before Fifth Army had closed up to the Gustav Line. On 21 December, following Clark's reluctant recommendation, Alexander had finally cancelled as too hazardous a projected landing in January behind the Gustav Line.[26] This was to have been at Anzio, some 35 miles to the south of Rome, where there was a small port and suitable beaches within range of Allied fighter cover. The landing force, based upon a single division, would be too weak to withstand a German reaction of the type experienced at Salerno. Fifth Army, moreover, would be in no position to offer any support; it was still fighting its way through the Bernhardt Line.

2
THROUGH THE BERNHARDT LINE

The Bernhardt Line, or to the Allies the Winter Line, was a series of defensive positions constructed around a natural bottleneck known as the Mignano Gap, where Highway 6 passed through a narrow valley dominated by surrounding heights. These were Monte Sammucro, Monte Lungo, and Monte Rotundo to the north, and Monte Maggiore, Monte la Difensa, and Monte Camino to the south. In some six weeks of unremitting attack from the beginning of December 1943 until the middle of January 1944, Fifth Army fought its way through these positions to reach the outposts of the Gustav Line. These actions typified the fighting in Italy, the forces involved and their tactical methods. They also proved to be only the overture to the main assault to reach the Liri Valley, and the first battle of Cassino, but this had not been Clark's intention.

The Fifth Army Plan
On 24 November Clark issued the operation instruction for his attack, the initial part of which was named 'Raincoat'. Fifth Army would first attack on the left of the Mignano Gap, then on the right, and finally through the centre to the Liri Valley. In the first phase, Lieutenant-General Richard McCreery's British X Corps on Fifth Army's left flank, and Major General Geoffrey Keyes' US II Corps in the centre, were to cooperate to capture the heights Monte Camino–Monte la Difensa–Monte Maggiore, forming the left shoulder of the Mignano Gap. On Fifth Army's right, Major General John Lucas' US VI Corps would harass the Germans along its front to draw in their reserves. With the same object, on Fifth Army's coastal flank Royal Navy warships would bombard the coast, and landing-craft make feints close inshore, as part of a deception scheme to convince the Germans of a seaborne landing in the Gulf of Gaeta.

With Monte Camino captured, and Monte la Difensa and Monte Maggiore secured by II Corps, X Corps would then feint a crossing of the lower reaches of the River Garigliano, and relieve II Corps for the second phase, the capture of Monte Sammucro. In this, II Corps would be assisted by the advance of VI Corps, and the latter was to push a division towards the mountains immediately to the north and north-west of Cassino. Once both shoulders of the Mignano gap were secure, Fifth Army could launch the third phase of its attack. In this, VI Corps would capture the heights behind Cassino, and X Corps would cross the Garigliano and advance along the coast. This would cover the flank of the II Corps' attack along Highway 6 towards Cassino which was intended to open the Liri Valley for an armoured breakthrough.

From interception of signals and aerial photographic reconnaissance, the Allied commanders were aware of the construction work in progress on the Gustav Line positions, and that time was imperative.[1] Yet, the terrain and the like-

> **FIFTH ARMY ORDER OF BATTLE FOR 'RAINCOAT'**
> A three-phase attack with three corps abreast on the Bernhardt Line, November 1943 to January 1944.[2]
>
> **Left flank:** British X Corps (46th and 56th Infantry Divisions)
> **Centre:** US II Corps (3rd and 36th Infantry Divisions, 1st Special Service Force,* 1st Italian Motorised Group)**
> **Right flank:** US VI Corps (34th and 45th Infantry Divisions, 2nd Moroccan Division*** replaced US 34th Division in December)
> **Army Reserve:** US 1st Armored Division
>
> * Six battalions of picked US and Canadian troops trained in mountain warfare and skiing, equipped with infantry weapons, 60mm mortars, flame-throwers and rocket-launchers. There was an attached battalion of US airborne artillery. The force had 1,200 vehicles including 1,000 Weasel tracked amphibious carriers useful for movement in hilly and snow-covered terrain.
> ** The first operational formation in Italy of the French Expeditionary Corps.
> *** Four battalions of Italian infantry with supporting field and anti-tank artillery.

lihood of resistance were heavily against Fifth Army's quickly clearing the Bernhardt Line and breaking through the Gustav Line, before its defences became too strong, to reach the Liri Valley and Rome. With the available routes commanded by strongly defended heights, Fifth Army's advance would be over difficult ground, with its progress and forward supply dependent upon infantry and pack animals. This alone would make rapid progress unlikely, but Fifth Army was also about to tackle the prospect in the appalling weather of a severe Italian winter.

Alexander scheduled the Fifth Army attack for 12 December, in the hope that Eighth Army's attack along the Sangro would have drawn further German troops to the Adriatic sector. This was not soon enough for Clark, however. He was concerned to gain ground from which to support the projected amphibious operation,

> **General Sir Harold Alexander:** Fifty-two years old in 1943, Alexander was a distinguished professional soldier of great personal charm and integrity. He commanded the rearguard at Dunkirk in 1940 and only left the beaches when satisfied that all troops had embarked. He later directed the retreat from Burma in 1942, successfully extricating the Burma Army from the threat of destruction by the Japanese. He was appointed Commander-in-Chief Middle East in August 1942, and later Deputy to General Eisenhower and Commander 18th Army Group, the Anglo-American armies in Tunisia. He commanded 15th Army Group, the Anglo-American armies during the invasion of Sicily and mainland Italy. At the end of 1943, on Eisenhower's return to Britain as Allied Supreme Commander for 'Overlord', Alexander became Commander-in-Chief Allied Forces in Italy. 'Alex' was a highly successful coalition commander, who earned the liking and respect of the various national contingents under his command. He was not a forceful man, however, and appears to have been incapable of imposing his will upon subordinate commanders. Described as self-effacing and sensitive, and 'too great a gentleman to hurt other men's feelings if he could avoid doing so',[3] Alexander depended upon a strong Chief of Staff both to ensure the firm grip of command and to develop fully the potential of his sound operational concepts.

> **General Mark W. Clark,** The young, at forty-seven years old, commander of the US Fifth Army, to which he was appointed in January 1943. Clark was Chief of Staff of the Army Ground Forces in 1942, and in November that year he made a courageous landing on the Algerian coast from a British submarine. This was in order to contact French officials in preparation for operation 'Torch', the allied landings in French North Africa. Clark remains a controversial figure. In Italy, he gained a reputation as publicity-conscious, at least partly because he was concerned that, in a British-dominated theatre, the exploits of his army would be deliberately played down in favour of the British Eighth Army. He faced the difficult task of simultaneously running both the Fifth Army attack on the Gustav Line and the Anzio landing. He has been criticised for encouraging Lucas to be cautious at Anzio and for ordering the disastrous assault over the Rapido River by the US 36th (Texas) Division. The latter was the subject of a Congressional Inquiry after the war, called for by the State of Texas, which exonerated Clark. The most controversial decision by Clark came after the Cassino battles, when he ordered the VI Corps breaking out from the Anzio beachhead to advance towards Rome, rather than as Alexander intended towards Valmontone. His determination to ensure that his Army should be the first to enter the Italian capital thus, arguably, prevented the intended entrapment and destruction of Kesselring's forces.

intended to unhinge the German defences south of Rome, while sufficient landing craft remained in theatre to make it feasible. He was also keen to ensure that his Army would capture the Italian capital. Time was critical, and he urged Alexander to allow Fifth Army to launch its attack at the beginning of December. Alexander agreed, but warned Clark that while he had been fighting rearguards since Salerno, he would now confront a determined German defence, and that he should avoid weakening Fifth Army by heavy losses in the Winter Line. Clark was sanguine: 'Don't worry,' he told Alexander, 'I'll get through the Winter Line all right and push the Germans out.'[4]

FIFTH ARMY AND FIREPOWER
Infantry
As with Eighth Army on the Adriatic sector, Fifth Army had learned that attacking in the terrain prevalent in Italy placed much of the burden of fighting upon the infantry. This burden fell particularly on the riflemen who constituted the combat cutting edge of a division, but only some 13 per cent of its full strength.[5] British infantry battalions comprised four rifle companies, their combined strength amounting to some 360 men in a total of twelve platoons, each platoon having three sections with, in each section, a Bren light machine gun. Each platoon was also equipped with a 2in mortar for fire support, and with a PIAT anti-tank projector that fired a 3lb anti-tank projectile. In each battalion, a further 340 men were employed either in supporting units or in non-combatant roles. A battalion's support company provided its principal firepower, with a carrier platoon with thirteen tracked Bren gun carriers, a mortar platoon with

	ALLIED INFANTRY DIVISIONS, 1944[6]		
	British	**United States**	**French (Expeditionary Corps in Italy)**
	Based on three Brigades each of three Battalions	Based on three Regiments each of three Battalions	Based on three Regiments each of three Battalions
Strength	18,347 (official)	14,253 (official)	14,000 (i.e. 2nd Moroccan Div effective strength May 1944)
Rifles	9,437	6,518	
Machine guns	1,322	636	
Mortars	359	144	French infantry divisions organised and equipped broadly on US lines.
Infantry anti-tank Weapons (British PIAT, US Bazooka)	436	557	French colonial light irregular infantry organised into Tabors (battalions) of four Goums (companies). Tabor strength: 924 (plus 274 mules)
Anti-tank guns	110	57	
Artillery (Medium and light guns)	72	66	Group of Tabors (Brigade) strength: 3,100
Vehicles	3,347	2,012	A Tabor included a Heavy Weapons Goum (mortars and machine-guns)

six 3in mortars, and an anti-tank platoon with six 6pdr anti-tank guns.[7] In US infantry battalions there were three rifle companies, each of three platoons of 36 riflemen and a support weapons platoon.

In Italy during 1943–44, the casualty rate among the riflemen in both US and British battalions was extremely heavy. In some British battalions in Fifth Army in late 1943 they averaged some 360 men, approximating to a battalion's actual rifle strength.[8] Both Fifth and Eighth armies faced the problem that priority in replacements went to other theatres and, particularly, the build-up in Britain for 'Overlord'. In early 1944, the replacement problem became critical for the British whose general manpower reserves after four years of war were fast depleting. In Italy, with a rate of battle attrition far exceeding the expected wastage, sometimes by 100 per cent, the rate of available reinforcements simply could not keep up and there was a particular shortage of junior officers. The break-up of divisions held in North Africa, a reduction in battalion establishments, and the disbanding of non-essential units could only partially compensate. In January 1944, the British divisions in Fifth Army's X Corps required

4,686 replacements, yet received only 219. In the following month the battalions in the British 1st and 56th Divisions in Fifth Army had respective strengths averaging only 590 and 554 against official establishments of 809.[9] In terms of rifle strength, they were close to becoming ineffective and Clark officially recorded his concern to Alexander. Heavy losses and too few replacements placed an even greater burden upon the remaining veterans in the rifle companies; they were rapidly diminishing assets, that could be replaced neither easily nor quickly.

Artillery

In 1944, a US Army study noted the increasing importance of artillery in mountain warfare because it was 'necessary literally to blow the enemy out of his mountain strong points'.[10] In its attack upon the Bernhardt Line, Fifth Army would depend heavily on supporting firepower to overcome German defences, and save infantry casualties. In Italy, the Allies were far superior to the Germans in artillery, and their reliance upon it was extremely heavy. In the British experience, for example, their artillery expended some 22,000 tons of ammunition per month between October and December 1943, compared with the 10,000 tons per month fired during the final eight months of the North African campaign, October 1942 to May 1943.[11] In Italy, both Eighth and Fifth Armies threatened to outrun their ammunition stocks and the rate of replenishment, and there were local shortages of artillery rounds before the end of 1943. Resupply problems in difficult mountainous terrain exacerbated this situation, but a British report in early 1944 expressed concern at the 'incredible ammunition expenditure' in Italy and at the rate of gun barrel and gun replacement.[12]

For 'Raincoat', Fifth Army's artillery support was lavish. In addition to its divisional artilleries, the British X Corps received 200 extra guns, and the US II Corps, an additional fourteen battalions of US field artillery. Fifth Army could also expect considerable air support. Although the Luftwaffe had not completely disappeared from Italian skies, it had less than 500 operational aircraft in theatre to set against the several thousand available to the Allies, who held unchallenged air superiority. The US XII Air Support Command's squadrons of single-engined fighter-bombers, supplemented by squadrons of twin-engined light bombers, prepared to support Fifth Army with an intensive bomb-

ALLIED ARTILLERY[13]		
Weapon	Range (yards)	Rate of Fire (rounds per minute)
British		
25-pdr gun/howitzer (principal field gun)	13,500	4
5.5in gun/howitzer	16,200	2
7.2in howitzer	16,900	1
US		
105mm howitzer	12,500	4
155mm gun	25,7156	1
155mm howitzer	16,000	2

ing programme against German front-line positions and rear area communications targets.[14] Their concern was not the Luftwaffe, but the deteriorating weather.

The Germans: Defensive Tactics

Despite Clark's optimism, the Germans had no intention of being pushed out of their Bernhardt Line positions easily. Kesselring's instructions to von Vietinghoff were for Tenth Army to hold its positions for as long as possible. In fact, throughout most of the fighting on the Bernhardt Line von Vietinghoff was on sick leave. From 5 November until his return on 28 December command of Tenth Army was held by General Joachim Lemelsen, who proved equally determined to obey Kesselring's injunction. Kesselring's instruction reflected not only his need for time to construct the more formidable Gustav Line, but also an increasing German reliance upon well-armed and heavily protected static defences. The principal reason for this was lack of troops, caused mainly by the continuous heavy attrition of the campaign in Russia, where some 165 of Germany's total of 236 divisions were committed. By the end of 1943, the OKW could call upon no readily deployable strategic reserve, and to provide significant reinforcements for one theatre meant denuding another. The ever-dwindling supply of replacements could not keep up with the rate of casualties and, in an attempt to make less go further, in October 1943 German infantry divisions were reorganised with fewer battalions.

Below: The commander of the German Tenth Army in Italy, General von Vietinghoff.

Until then, German infantry divisions comprised, in addition to their anti-tank and reconnaissance battalions, three infantry regiments each with three rifle battalions. The October 1943 reorganisation downsized the infantry regiments to two rifle battalions, reducing divisional establishment from some 17,000 to 13,500 men. Organic artillery firepower, usually a medium regiment of 150mm howitzers supplemented by light battalions of 105mm guns or howitzers, remained intact. Such establishment figures are quite meaningless, however, when considering the actual strength of German divisions at this stage of the war. Combat wastage and the difficulty in finding replacements meant that battalions often amounted to little more than strong companies, and a battalion that had a fighting strength of four hundred was considered good, but unusual.[15] Panzer Grenadier divisions differed from those of line infantry in having two regiments of three battalions in armoured half-track personnel carriers, along with artillery and engineers who, in the German army, were frequently used as combat troops, and a tank battalion. In the fighting in Italy, offering little scope for the mass use of armour, the Germans considered these divisions a more useful combination than the full panzer division, though they were never at anything approaching full strength in manpower or equipment. Kesselring was in no doubt that his strength in combat troops was finite; in December 1943 the OKW informed him that he must economise manpower in Italy, and that his watchword must be 'build, build, and keep on building'.[16]

The XIV Panzer Corps, commanded by General Fridolin von Senger und Etterlin, held the Bernhardt positions opposite Fifth Army with some five divisions. These were by no means at full strength, and all their infantry battalions were committed in the front-line positions, with their reconnaissance battalions as immediate reserve. They had the advantage of ground well suited to defence, and they had demolished the bridges, and mined the roads, tracks and stream beds to slow Fifth Army's advance and deployment. Their positions contained numerous strongly constructed bunkers, and there were many dug-in machine-gun and mortar emplacements. The high ground gave them good observation for their artillery, though in this they could not match Fifth Army's firepower. A Fifth Army Intelligence report of late November estimated German artillery strength on its sector as only some 216 guns, though with some additional batteries and long-range guns located well to the rear.[17] Nor could XIV Panzer Corps expect any air support.

General Fridolin von Senger und Etterlin, fifty-two years old, was a highly experienced operational commander by the time he took command of the XIV Panzer Corps in October 1943. He had commanded a cavalry brigade in the invasion of the west in 1940, and later commanded the 17th Panzer Division on the Eastern Front during the attempt to relieve the Sixth Army trapped at Stalingrad. During the summer of 1943, von Senger was the liaison officer between the German and Italian forces defending Sicily, and subsequently he directed the evacuation of German troops from Corsica and Sardinia. Von Senger proved a skilful defensive commander and in January 1944 he was promoted to Panzer General. He was an Oxford Rhodes scholar and a lay member of the Benedictine Order, and became increasingly disillusioned with the Nazi regime that he served.

> **GERMAN XIV PANZER CORPS (TENTH ARMY)**[18]
> Order of Battle Bernhardt Line position, November 1943 to January 1944
> *(Figures in parentheses are known fighting strengths reported 9 December)*
>
> *Opposite British X and US II Corps*
> 15th Panzer Grenadier Division (6,660): Monte Maggiore – la Difensa – Monte Camino
> 94th Infantry Division (7,430): Monte Fuga – Castelforte – along River Garigliano to sea.
>
> *Opposite US II Corps*
> 29th Panzer Grenadier Division (7,460): Monte Corno – Monte Sammucro – San Pietro Infine – Monte Lungo
>
> *Opposite US VI Corps*
> 305th Infantry Division (6,700): Isernia – Castel di Sangro-Atina
> 44th Infantry Division: Venafro – Filignano.
>
> **Tenth Army Reserve:** Hermann Goering Panzer Division (Grenadier regiments in Bernhardt Line, some elements working on Gustav Line defences).

The XIV Panzer Corps could not afford heavy attrition of its infantry. Although holding well-protected positions could reduce the vulnerability of troops, fighting on the defensive involved far more than this. To maintain an effective defence while retaining the initiative in battle depended upon the capability to counter-attack. At this, the Germans were particularly adept and a favoured tactic was the immediate counter-attack, timed to catch Allied troops off balance when they had just captured, but not consolidated, their objective. Often preceded by a sharp artillery barrage or heavy mortaring, and sometimes supported by tanks or light armour when available, these attacks could be devastatingly effective, especially against tired or unseasoned troops. They often resulted in the recapture of the ground lost. Such tactics were not always successful, however, and even when they were the cost could be prohibitive because they necessarily risked exposure to the usually superior Allied firepower. German troops caught in the open by rapid and responsive artillery concentrations, at which the Allied artillery became proficient, were decimated. Experienced Allied formations ensured that their artillery covered all likely counter-attack approaches, and selected objectives inviting counter-attack over ground favourable to their artillery. The US 34th Infantry Division, for example, reported in 1944 the effectiveness of this practice, referring to such ground as 'the murder space'.[19]

Yet for the Germans, to counter-attack was essential, and they had little option but to risk the consequent casualties. Kesselring's instructions to Tenth Army in the Bernhardt Line stipulated that withdrawal to the Gustav Line was permissible only when such casualties ceased to be proportional to the tactical successes gained.

Mountain Warfare

With few exceptions, notably the Indian divisions in Eighth Army and the North African divisions of the French Expeditionary Corps, the officers and men of the Allied armies in Italy were neither prepared for nor experienced in mountain warfare. They had to learn, through harsh combat experience, to become mountain warriors. This was not just a question of learning how to move, and fight, in mountainous terrain, but of developing the skills and experience necessary to identify the potential of ground and exploit it. It took time and so too did the physical hardening necessary to survive, let alone fight, in the mountains during winter. For mechanised armies trained for, and experienced in, mobile operations on level ground exploiting firepower and movement, the mountains in Italy were not only physical but psychological obstacles. They could not be easily bypassed, they had to be overcome, and Allied commanders found many of the weapons upon which their operations hitherto had relied, tanks, concentrated artillery and air support, could not be employed in the same way, if they could be employed at all. The imperative became to overcome these obstacles quickly, in order to exploit the full strength of their armies and return to tried and familiar methods. With very few exceptions – General Alphonse Juin commanding the French Expeditionary Corps was one – mountainous terrain was not thought of as an operational context that could be utilised and exploited in an offensive.[20] The Germans in Italy were in the same predicament. Although they held and ably exploited the defender's advantage of terrain, this did not mean that they possessed the advantage of being skilled mountain soldiers. They were not, and this became quite apparent when they faced those who were, such as Juin's Moroccans and Algerians. In fact, German divisions were no better equipped or specifically trained for the mountains than their opponents. Kesselring initially hoped to have German mountain divisions sent to Italy, but they were committed, and had been for some time, on the Eastern Front from where they could be neither disengaged nor transferred easily. Moreover, fighting on the plains of Russia gave them no opportunity or incentive to retain or develop the skills associated with their title. In late 1943, Kesselring obtained the 5th Mountain Division from the Finnish sector of the Eastern Front, but as a German veteran of Italy and military historian later commented, it 'had long since forgotten all it had ever known about mountain warfare'.[21]

Fighting in the mountains and gaining experience of German defensive techniques compelled the Allied infantry divisions to develop specific tactics. Generally, they had to seize dominating heights, while avoiding movement through the valleys or along the most natural avenues of approach that were invariably mined and covered by machine-guns and mortars. Instead they had to work their way up the high ridges and slopes, and then down to prise the Germans from their positions. It was along the slopes that much close-quarter fighting occurred, involving small units and strong fighting patrols, with automatic weapons and grenades heavily used, though there are frequent references to the bayonet. Allied troops found that such fighting meant taking one German-held feature at a time, often to find that the ground they had captured was untenable because it was covered by the guns of adjacent features that had to be taken in their turn. It was not unusual for Allied troops to secure a height, only to come under immediate and often devastating mortar and artillery fire from such adjacent positions. Allied troops also learned that the Germans excelled in rear-slope defence, often deploying only a thin screen along forward slopes. With their main strength along rear-slope positions, often not observable to Allied artillery spotters, they could bring heavy and effective fire on the attackers as they came over the crests, and mount sharp and rapid counter-attacks.

There were few 'short-cuts' in mountain fighting. To avoid the obvious and dangerous approaches by outflanking German positions often meant extreme exertion, climbing and sometimes crawling, perhaps for hours. Then, the skills necessary to overcome German positions depended upon basic infantry principles sharpened and adapted to the terrain; thorough reconnaissance, the effective use of cover and concealment to achieve surprise, maintaining control over the attacking units, and the ensuring of co-ordination between the assault troops and their supporting heavier machine-guns and mortars and, when available, supporting artillery. With much of the movement and fighting taking place at night, to avoid observation and achieve surprise, the importance of small-unit leadership became critical.

Success in the attack ultimately depended upon the Allied troops closing the German positions and clearing them. This was where close fire support could be decisive, but in ground where artillery fire could not be called down, even when available, the attacking troops were dependent upon their own weapons, and particularly their mortars. As a US Army report later acknowledged, in the high mountain areas, with large areas of dead ground and defiladed German positions inaccessible to artillery fire, mortars became essential support weapons.[22] Many strongly constructed German bunker and cave positions were impervious to even a direct hit by an artillery shell or mortar bomb. Allied troops learnt to approach them under the cover of mortar fire, finally rushing in to attack as the fire lifted and, with luck, catching the Germans just emerging to man their fire positions. The problem was that, as with everything else in the mountains, the troops had to carry their mortars and ammunition by mules or by hand, so the quantity of rounds was limited, and resupply difficult. American companies in Fifth Army found that it was impracticable to carry forward more than two of their 81mm mortars in an attack, and that these would use up all the rounds that could be carried for them. As one infantry company commander put it, 'It is much better to have two mortars firing when you need them than to have six mortars without ammunition.'[23]

When attacks petered out through exhaustion or impossible weather, there were long periods of static warfare. Both sides dug-in. Often Allied and German positions remained very close, within grenade-throwing range, their occupants dependent upon supplies brought up by porters or mules. In winter, this debilitating existence in the extreme cold and wet was a severe test of stamina and endurance. For both sides, the conditions of living and fighting mirrored those of the trench warfare of the First World War. The same incapacitating conditions and consequences also reappeared, such as 'trench foot', atrophy of the feet due to prolonged immersion in water. Both sides patrolled aggressively, and Allied troops had to contend with German infiltration and sniping, often from cave positions, previously prepared and well hidden, and which the Allied troops could not easily locate.

Raincoat: The Offensive
'Raincoat' opened at the beginning of December as British X Corps' 46th and 56th Divisions attacked Monte Camino, supported by an initial bombardment by 820 guns against known or suspected German positions. They fired at least 165,000 rounds, high-explosive, white phosphorus and smoke, with such a weight of fire that some targets received eleven tons of high-explosive per minute. Thereafter, concentrations of at least 300 guns placed fire on targets as requested by the attacking battalions. The aim was to destroy the German positions and to suppress defensive fire; in fact German troops well dug-in actually suffered few casualties from this storm of steel, but they were pinned to their positions, unable to mount local counter-attacks, and they were isolated from reinforcement and supply. This was also an important contribution of the supporting bombers and fighter-bombers of XII Air Support Command, who flew nearly 1,000 sorties on the first two days of the attack. Most of these were against German positions immediately ahead of the attacking troops, though the pilots reported that a combination of poor weather, mountainous terrain and German camouflage hampered accurate target identification. On the ground, the Allied gunners also had their troubles. Their guns lacked sufficient elevation to engage some mountain targets and movement was difficult, the heavier guns frequently sinking into the clinging mud from which only winches could retrieve them.

Late on 1 December, the 139th Brigade of 46th Division attacked the village of Calabritto on the lower slopes of Camino; this was diversionary, intended to engage German attention while securing the jumping-off points for 56th Division on the right. Under heavy machine-gun fire, the attacking battalions struggled all night to break through the barbed wire and minefields in their path, and by dawn were within 200 yards of the village. Supporting tanks tried to shoot the infantry into the village by engaging the stone houses covering German strongpoints, but to no avail, the positions of the 129th Panzer Grenadier Regiment being too strong. Enough ground was secured, however, for 56th Division, whose 169th and 167th Brigades late on 2 December made a night attack on the two ridges leading to the crest of Monte Camino, held by three battalions of the 15th Panzer Grenadier Division. Initially, and despite a

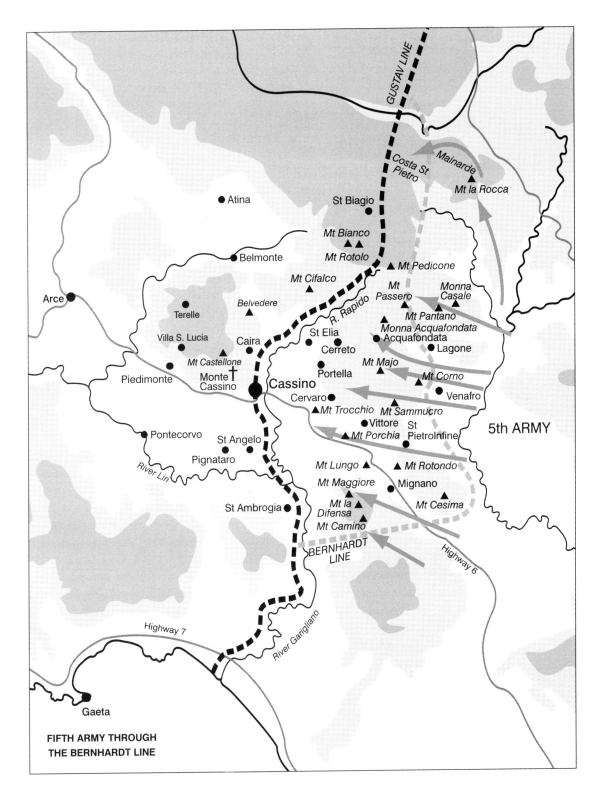

difficult climb over loose stones and boulder-strewn ground that inevitably slowed momentum, they made good progress and reached the crest. Then began the German counter-attacks, and by 5 December a further three panzer grenadier battalions had been fed into the battle, including two from the Hermann Goering Panzer Division. The crest of Monte Camino fell finally late on 6 December, after prolonged fighting in which the British and German troops had attacked and counter-attacked successively, and in which the crest changed hands twice. For both sides, this was a confusing battle. The XIV Panzer Corps was unsure whether the forward battalion of 15th Panzer Grenadiers were still in possession of the summit, following reports by troops on the rear slope that they could still see German troops there. Only when a runner, sent to investigate, returned was the uncertainty removed – the men that could be seen were corpses.[24] Three days later, X Corps had cleared the western part of the Camino position to the River Garigliano, some eighteen British battalions being engaged, and it had cost them 941 casualties. Despite fighting on the defensive, 15th Panzer Grenadiers' own casualties were higher at 974,[25] a likely reflection on the ferocity of its counter-attacks. What was becoming all too clear in this fighting was the necessity for the utmost physical conditioning and hardening of the infantrymen, if they were to stand up to the continual strain of fighting in the mountains in winter. The bitter cold, the incessant rain that kept clothes and bedding damp, and the thick, pervading mud all took their toll of health. A US Army report later acknowledged that 'only the highest level of hardening and stamina can resist the physical strain of combat operations under these conditions'.[26]

To the north-east, in the US II Corps sector, Colonel Robert T. Frederick's élite 1st Special Service Force had captured most of la Difensa by dawn on 3 December, gaining surprise after a hazardous night ascent over precipitous and trackless ground. Then, for several days during which the troops received few supplies and had little shelter from accurate mortar and artillery fire and the icy wind, fog and incessant rain, they successfully held off counter-attacks. It was a battle of fierce small-scale actions, in which opposing patrols would encounter each other in the fog and fight hand-to-hand on the narrow ledges. With the British capture of Camino the German pressure eased, but Frederick's force had by then 511 casualties, including 116 requiring hospitalisation from sheer physical exhaustion. Three days' rest, Frederick reckoned, were necessary before a man returning from la Difensa was fit again for action.[27]

In the meantime, two battalions of the 142nd Infantry, of General Walker's 36th Division, having partly followed the Special Service troops ascending la Difensa, turned off to attack the Monte Maggiore ridge which they quickly secured through rapidly following their artillery support. Thereafter, while remaining under German mortar and artillery fire, their problem became really one of supply. This was the severest obstacle to maintaining an advance or sustaining troops over long distance in harsh terrain. As the troops penetrated into the high mountains, where no wheeled vehicle could go, their supplies of food rations, water and ammunition became dependent upon pack-mule columns and manhandling, or air supply when the terrain and weather allowed.[28] The predicament of the 142nd Infantry on the Maggiore ridge was acute, for not even mules could negotiate the mountain tracks in the heavy rain, along the steepest of which men could only crawl through the mud dragging their packs with ropes to reach the forward positions. Fighter-bomber pilots attempted to help by dropping supplies but it was no use; both the nature of the ground and the weather defeated their efforts. The only way of keeping the 142nd's companies on the Maggiore ridge supplied was for half the regiment, plus two companies of the 141st Infantry, to act as porters, who made arduous three-mile round trips that took twelve hours.[29] The Germans were in the same predicament, and often worse as Allied air and artillery firepower prevented the forward movement of supplies and reliefs.

In the US VI Corps sector, the 34th and 45th Divisions had, since 29 November, attacked in the direction of Atina and San Elia, along the axes of narrow roads overlooked by hills. The Germans opposite them, of the 44th and 305th Divisions, fought stubbornly from well-sited positions, and VI Corps made little headway, though it was undoubtedly pinning the German reserves as intended. By 8 December, both the US divisions were exhausted. The 34th alone had sustained 800 casualties, and Lucas relieved it in the line by the 2nd Moroccan Division, newly arrived in Italy, and the first formation of General Alphonse Juin's French Expeditionary Corps to become operational with Fifth Army.

Despite the determined defence, the rain, the bitter cold, and the mountains, Fifth Army had broken into the Bernhardt Line; it had yet to break through it. The second phase of Fifth Army's attack intended to open Highway 6 where it ran through a valley a mile wide between Monte Sammucro and Monte Lungo, with the terraced village of San Pietro Infine lying just north of the road and partly along the slope of Monte Sammucro. Here occurred some of the hardest fighting of the Bernhardt Line, as US II Corps fought to capture these two heights and pinch out the Germans from San Pietro and the valley.

Fifth Army's Intelligence staff at first considered a determined German defence of San Pietro and Monte Lungo unlikely. Monte Lungo appeared dominated by Monte Maggiore, expected to be firmly in American hands, and Monte Sammucro seemed to be lightly held by the Germans, if at all. An advance westward along the southern slopes of Sammucro to Highway 6 would clear San Pietro and isolate Monte Lungo, and hasten a German withdrawal over the rivers Rapido and Garigliano. This was optimistic, to say the least, and reveals a paucity of knowledge both of German dispositions and the nature of the ground. In fact, by mid-November Kesselring and Lemelsen, their freedom of action removed by Hitler's direct intervention, knew that San Pietro must be held. Covering this sector by early December were two regiments of the 29th Panzer Grenadier Division, one holding Monte Lungo and the other Monte Sammucro, plus a weakened regiment of the 3rd Panzer Grenadier Division. A battalion of panzer grenadiers held San Pietro, occupying what amounted to a fortress. The thick stone walls of the village buildings offered superb emplacements, and the village, with excellent observation of Monte Lungo and Highway 6 and bordered by the road and a deep gully, could only be entered by means of the tracks across Monte Sammucro.

At the end of November and beginning of December patrols by Walker's 36th Division and its attached 3rd Ranger Battalion probed San Pietro. Apart from learning the hard way that the Germans had strong artillery and mortar support, they could gain no firm indications of strength or dispositions, though at least one patrol reported the village full of German troops. Walker and his Corps Commander, Keyes, planned an attack using two battalions of the 143rd Infantry to capture the high ground of Monte Sammucro to the north and west of San Pietro and take the village from the rear. The Rangers would capture Hill 950, on the east of Monte Sammucro, maintaining contact with VI Corps on their right. Keyes also attached General Dupino's Italian 1st Motorised Group to Walker's 36th Division, with the object of capturing Monte Lungo. This would be the first action of Italian troops under Allied command since Badoglio's declaration of war against Germany in October. Therefore there was much concern that it should be successful; Keyes went to considerable length to ensure that the Italians had adequate fire support, and insisted that their task should be well within their capabilities.

The II Corps attack began late on 7 December as three battalions of the 143rd Infantry and the 3rd Ranger Battalion made their two-pronged attack on the Monte Sammucro position. On the northern part of Sammucro, the attacks went well and secured the crest early on 8 December. There followed a ferocious reaction, this time by the 29th Panzer Grenadier Division's 71st Grenadier Regiment, whose counter-attacks lasted for the next four days. On the southern part of Sammucro near San Pietro, the attack made no progress. The 143rd Infantry's 2nd Battalion made 400 yards before being held by a storm of artillery, mortar and machine-gun fire. Despite further attempts, and Allied artillery pounding and reducing San Pietro to rubble, the situation remained unchanged for days. The Italian attack on Monte Lungo promised well but met similar and unexpected resistance which soon broke up the compact formation in which the Italians, ill-advisedly, had marched up the hill. Confusion, disorganisation and demoralisation soon set in and the attack collapsed with the Italians falling back upon US positions, having suffered over 300 casualties. On Sammucro the heavy fighting had worn down the strength of the US battalions alarmingly. Clark attached to II Corps the 504th Parachute Infantry, a timely reinforcement that ensured the holding of Sammucro, but also indicated the toll that the Bernhardt Line was exacting.

The next move was a further attempt against Sammucro and San Pietro, this time using tanks. Although well aware that the terrain was hardly suitable, Walker was persuaded to employ a small force of them, not least because Clark, who had secured the US 1st Armored Division for Fifth Army, was keen to see armour employed. The attempt was made on 15 December, with Sherman tanks of the 36th Division's attached 753rd Tank Battalion, but failed after two days' fighting in which the US infantry again suffered heavily and, although breaking into the village and clearing some strongpoints with bayonet and grenade, were forced out again. Despite the determined ingenuity of the tank officers and engineers in devising and attempting various methods whereby the tanks could negotiate the terraces in order to support the infantry with their fire, the tanks actually proved of little help. With the single narrow road mined and the surrounding ground either too sodden or steeply terraced and enclosed, they remained unable to manoeuvre, lacked sufficient visibility, and were vulnerable to German fire. Sixteen Sherman medium tanks were deployed, along with a British Valentine bridge-laying tank borrowed from X Corps to help negotiate the ground; all but four Shermans were destroyed or disabled.[30]

Monte Lungo, however, fell on 16 December to a pincer attack from Monte Maggiore. It was this, in combination with the progress of the US VI Corps to the north, that began to loosen the German grip on San Pietro that was unshakeable by direct attack. Lucas' VI Corps was pressing the Germans on its front and was slowly advancing in the general direction of Atina and the heights north and north-west of Cassino. By 15 December the US 45th Division reached Lagone, having penetrated the defences on the front of the German 44th Infantry Division. Farther north, the 2nd Moroccan Division of the French Expeditionary Corps threatened the positions of the German 305th Infantry Division between Monte La Rocca and Monte Pantano. In their first action in Italy the Moroccans, with their French officers and NCOs, were proving themselves able and ferocious mountain fighters, capable of a phenomenal rate of advance in such terrain. In fact, they were helping to turn the northern flank of XIV Panzer Corps, much to the concern of Kesselring and von Senger. With the reluctant assent of Hitler, who had ordered a stand-fast, Kesselring sanctioned a pull-back by the 44th Infantry and 29th Panzer Grenadier Divisions, and on 17 December, US patrols found San Pietro uncannily silent; the Germans had gone. San Pietro had cost the 36th Division some 1,200 casualties, including about 150 killed, over 800 wounded and some 250 missing.[31] It was a grim portent.

The end of the year saw the XIV Panzer Corps being squeezed out of the Bernhardt Line. It was falling back, but only slowly and stubbornly, and there was no possibility of an immediate thrust by Fifth Army into the Liri Valley. In fact, XIV Panzer Corps had received some reinforcement in the shape of 5th Mountain Division, and this allowed Kesselring to pull the 29th Panzer Grenadier Division out of the line for an overdue rest and re-equipment. The 5th Mountain Division was allotted the northern flank of the XIV Panzer Corps, which now held positions along the River Pecchia; Monte Porchia and Monte Trocchio to the south of Highway 6, and Monte Majo to the north. Here it would fight a further delaying action before withdrawing into the Gustav Line itself.

THE TIME IMPERATIVE
FIFTH ARMY AND 'SHINGLE'

In early January 1944, VI Corps was withdrawn from the Fifth Army front line and placed into reserve. Responsibility for its sector became that of General Alphonse Juin and his newly activated French Expeditionary Corps, whose 3rd Algerian Division had now arrived to join 2nd Moroccan Division in Fifth Army. Lucas and his Corps were to prepare for Operation 'Shingle', for the Allies had no intention now of trying to reach Rome by a direct assault upon the Gustav Line alone. They intended also to outflank it, from the sea.

The 'Shingle' concept emerged in Allied planning during the autumn of 1943, when it became apparent that there would be no rapid advance to Rome in the wake of a retreating German army. An amphibious landing behind their defensive lines was the obvious alternative to what was otherwise going to be at best a difficult and costly advance through the length of southern and central Italy, or at worst, a stalemate. The Germans certainly thought so. Kesselring recorded his conviction at the time that the Allied attacks with their 'reckless expenditure of troops' were not merely intended to pin down his forces. He believed they concealed an ulterior objective; the launching of a major offensive combined with a landing operation, most likely in the Rome region, and that to counter it he would need strong mobile reserves.[1]

Unknown to Kesselring, a severe shortage of shipping in the Mediterranean denied the Allies this option for a considerable period of time. From September 1943, Allied vessels were working to the limit of their capacity to build-up and keep supplied the Fifth and Eighth Armies. They also shipped to Italy the ground staffs and equipment of the Allied air forces, including the heavy bomber groups of the US Fifteenth Army Air Force transferred to airfields near Foggia for the Combined Bomber Offensive against Germany. This was a particularly heavy demand on shipping, and was met only at the expense of building-up the Fifth and Eighth Armies. Then, in October, began the withdrawal from the Mediterranean of specialist assault craft for 'Overlord', according to the rigid timetable agreed at the Trident and Quadrant conferences.

By December, it was apparent that there would be shipping available only for an assault landing behind the Gustav Line by a single division. As Alexander appreciated, this force would not be enough, either to shake the Germans out of their defence lines south of Rome or to withstand the likely speed and strength of their reaction, such as they had demonstrated at Salerno. Fifth Army would have to link up with such a landing force very rapidly indeed to prevent its destruction. The terrain and the strength of German positions on the Fifth Army front made it impossible for Fifth Army to reach the Frosinone area, at which time the landing was to take place. Consequently, on 21 December, following

Opposite page: Monte Cassino under aerial bombardment. The monastery can be discerned on Monte Cassino and, to the left of the bomb bursts on the slopes can be seen the hairpin bends on the road leading up to it. Cassino town, already heavily battered, is in the centre foreground. Entering the Rapido Valley from the bottom left and beginning to wind around Monte Cassino is Highway 6, which can also be discerned in the top left in the Liri Valley itself.

37

Clark's reluctant recommendation, Alexander cancelled as too hazardous the projected landing behind the Gustav Line.

By this time, concern about the lack of progress in Italy was evident among the Allied leaders, and particularly Churchill. Instead of celebrating Christmas 1943 in Rome, as he had told Eisenhower they would, he spent it in Carthage recovering from a severe bout of pneumonia contracted after the Tehran conference with President Roosevelt and the Russian leader, Marshal Joseph Stalin. Nevertheless, he was still the driving force behind the Italian campaign, the apparent stagnation of which he deplored and determined to alter by throwing his weight behind a renewed push for an amphibious 'left hook' behind the German lines. On Christmas Day, he presided over a meeting of senior Mediterranean commanders, including Alexander and Eisenhower, who was shortly to leave the theatre to assume supreme command of 'Overlord'. The meeting concluded that a landing to outflank the Gustav Line and open the road to Rome required a corps of at least two divisions with supporting armour and artillery. Churchill then signalled Roosevelt asking his agreement to a further delay in the withdrawal of the 56 British assault ships from the Mediterranean to allow a landing in the Anzio area on about 20 January. The prize was Rome, and the avoidance of a stalemate in Italy that would embarrass the Anglo-Americans in their relationship with Stalin, particularly as 'Overlord' remained several months away. Roosevelt agreed, providing the timetable for 'Overlord' remained unaffected.[2] 'Shingle', the amphibious 'left hook' at Anzio, was reborn and went into firm planning. Alexander, who became Commander-in-Chief of the Allied Armies in Italy on Eisenhower's departure,[3] prepared for what he termed the 'Battle for Rome', that was confidently expected to see the Allies in the Italian capital by February.

It was to be Clark's battle. His Fifth Army would be responsible for the combination of 'Shingle' and the linked assault on the Gustav Line. The backbone of Lucas' 'Shingle' force was to be the British 1st and US 3rd Infantry Divisions, reflecting Alexander's determination that the risks involved should be shared equally between allies.[4] Lucas would also have three US Ranger and two British Commando battalions, a regiment of parachute infantry and a Combat Command of the US 1st Armored Division.[5] Alexander decided on 22 January as the date for the 'Shingle' landings, within the tight time-frame dictated by the shipping constraints. His directive emphasised that the momentum of advance 'must be maintained at all costs to the limit of our resources. The enemy will be compelled to react to the threat to his communications and rear, and advantage must be taken of this to break through his main defences',[6] in order to achieve the earliest possible link-up between Fifth Army and the landing force. This meant that Fifth Army would have to attack the Gustav Line in strength several days before 'Shingle', to draw German reserves away from the landing area. It would then have to force a breach through the Liri Valley to enable the link-up with the seaborne force. At the same time, Eighth Army, now commanded by

General Sir Oliver Leese following Montgomery's return to Britain for 'Overlord', would attack on the Adriatic front to prevent the Germans transferring reinforcements from that sector. Clark's problem, therefore, and a considerable one, was time. His divisions that had fought through the Bernhardt Line were still fighting their way towards the Gustav Line in early January, as 'Shingle' was being prepared. They could have no respite for rest or redeployment, or for detailed reconnaissance of the ground and German positions, before tackling the Gustav Line in a frontal attack.

Nevertheless, there was considerable confidence about the forthcoming battle at Alexander's Fifteenth Army Group headquarters and within Fifth Army. On 16 January Fifth Army produced an Intelligence Summary that subsequent events would render infamous. Observing that German strength was ebbing on the Fifth Army front, it doubted whether the Germans, lacking fresh reserves, could hold their defensive line through Cassino against a coordinated army attack. Such an attack by Fifth Army was forthcoming, to be followed shortly afterwards by 'Shingle'. The Fifth Army Intelligence staff, reflecting the view of the senior Allied leadership, believed that once the magnitude of the threat posed by the landings became clear to the Germans, they would have no choice but to withdraw from the Gustav Line.[7] Although later scorned by historians, at the time this assessment, though optimistic, was not entirely baseless.

Through intercepts on a near daily basis, Allied signals intelligence through 'Ultra' kept the Allies informed about the strength and dispositions of Kesselring's forces in Italy. These intercepts in early January revealed German reports of the heavy casualties sustained in the fighting against Fifth Army, and the necessity of units falling back to new positions.[8] It was a picture of an army under severe pressure, suffering heavily, and maintaining its defence with difficulty. In the run-up to 'Shingle', there was also intense monitoring of the Tenth Army south of Rome and of the German forces in the Rome area itself. This indicated the presence of two parachute divisions in Rome under a new headquarters, that of I Parachute Corps. Near Rome were recuperating the veteran 90th and 29th Panzer Grenadier Divisions with about 100 tanks and assault guns between them. The immediate Anzio area was unguarded, and the main Fifth Army attack against the Gustav Line was intended to keep it that way,[9] by drawing these formations south and committing them to battle. There seemed a good chance for 'Shingle' to achieve surprise and knock the Germans off balance, though in this it amounted to a gamble with a strong element of bluff. Churchill spoke of hurling a 'wild cat' onto the Italian shore, since Lucas' VI Corps, after an unopposed landing, was intended to strike out boldly and aggressively towards Rome. Only by cutting the communications of XIV Panzer Corps to the south and giving an impression of greater strength than it actually possessed, could VI Corps alarm and confuse the Germans into withdrawing from the Gustav Line. Moreover, VI Corps would have to act quickly, immediately on landing, for if the Germans were caught with the door to Rome open, they must be allowed no opportunity to close it and avert crisis on the Gustav Line. In all its aspects, 'Shingle' was time-driven.

There was, however, a serious problem with 'Shingle', present even before it took place, and that would ultimately influence the entire battle for Rome. Between Alexander's concept and Churchill's expectation, and what Lucas and his immediate Army commander, Clark, intended, there existed a dangerously wide gulf. If ever a commander embarked upon an operation in which he lacked faith and was convinced of its likely failure, that man was Lucas. He described himself before 'Shingle' as 'a lamb being led to the slaughter'.[10] He had little confidence in Fifth Army advancing from the south to reach his beachhead quickly. This was not surprising given his experience of stubborn German fighting in the Bernhardt Line, and he had experienced at first hand the speed and strength of the German reaction to the Salerno landings. He was seriously concerned at the lack of time for adequate preparation for 'Shingle', and his concern was to get ashore and stay there, and certainly not to take risks. That Clark was content to entrust 'Shingle' to Lucas is explained only by the fact that he too was concerned primarily with VI Corps establishing and holding a beachhead, rather than striking inland. He told Lucas not to 'stick his neck out' as he himself had done at Salerno, and advised him to make adequate defensive preparations on landing in order to withstand counter-attacks. His operation order for 'Shingle' was ambiguous. After securing a beachhead VI Corps was to advance 'on' the Alban Hills, without specifying whether VI Corps should reach them or just advance towards them; Clark intended Lucas to use his own judgement after the landings, based on the extent of German opposition. Clark's ambiguity reflected the acute dilemma with which 'Shingle' confronted him. A single reinforced corps remained a weak force to land some 70 miles behind the German lines, and with strong German reaction its failure to secure its beachhead lifeline would mean its destruction. With 'Overlord' only months away, no one could contemplate with equanimity the military and political ramifications of an Allied seaborne landing being defeated by the Germans, least of all the Army commander responsible. Yet, for Clark to encourage Lucas to be cautious, who needed no such encouragement, was to stack further the odds against his main Fifth Army offensive. It would be against the entire spirit of the original 'Shingle' concept, for if Lucas were to shake the Gustav Line, he would have to do a lot more than get ashore and build a defensive perimeter.

Both Clark's Fifth Army Field Order for 'Shingle', issued on 12 January, and Lucas' subsequent Corps order reflected the emphasis on securing and establishing a strong beachhead. This was militarily sound, for it was expecting a great deal of a single corps to establish a beachhead, at the same time reach the Alban Hills, and hold them against counter-attack. Yet, not to accept the risks inherent with 'Shingle', meant to allow a possibly fleeting opportunity to pass. It also reflected considerable optimism that the Fifth Army attack on the Gustav Line would be successful, as breaking through to the Liri Valley and Rome now depended more upon this than upon 'Shingle', inverting the original concept. Alexander's own Operation Instruction to Fifth Army on 12 January stated that 'Shingle' was to 'cut the enemy's main communications in the Colli Laziali (Alban Hills) area south-east of Rome, and to threaten the rear of the German XIV Corps.'[11] Had Alexander but known it, the bulk of VI Corps' supporting armour, upon which this interpretation of 'Shingle' depended, was not even scheduled to be put ashore at Anzio until D plus six.[12]

The Bernhardt Line fighting suggested, however, that German resistance was beginning to crack, and that a sufficiently strong and determined attack would see Fifth Army through the Gustav Line. Clark, in line with Alexander's injunction to maintain attack momentum, determined to keep the Germans under pressure, though it could only be by pushing Fifth Army to the limit. Despite the terrain and weather conditions, his troops were showing remarkable stamina; the problem was that this stamina was being used up rapidly.

Firepower: German mortars supporting Heidrich's 1st Parachute Division preparing to fire from a position amid the ruins of Cassino. Note the camouflage smocks and rimless helmets of the parachute troops.

Mountain Warfare: Closing to the Gustav Line

At the turn of the year, a heavy blizzard had ground Fifth Army's advance to a temporary halt. There followed further snowfalls, a thaw, then bursts of heavy rain, mists, and freezing winds. The conditions in the mountains were appalling. In spite of them, on 5 January, the offensive resumed against XIV Panzer Corps' positions along the Peccia. The main striking force was again Keyes' II Corps. On the right, after an arduous approach march over gullies and slopes covered with snow and ice, the 1st Special Service Force reached positions from which on the night of 6/7 January they led off a two-pronged attack on Monte Majo and the nearby Monte Vischiataro. Monte Majo fell on the 7th, but counter-attacks by two battalions of the German 44th Infantry Division continued for the next three days, during which time some German and American positions remained within grenade-throwing range of one another.

Monte Vischiataro fell on 8 January, outflanked from Monte Majo. The US 34th Division, transferred from VI Corps to II Corps to relieve the 36th, attacked towards San Vittore and Cervaro, also on the front of the German 44th Division. San Vittore fell on 6 January to the 135th Infantry after some sharp house-to-house fighting. Cervaro fell to the 168th Infantry on 12 January, after a pounding by artillery and a close support strike by A-36 fighter-bombers. On 11 January, an observation officer with the 168th Infantry witnessed this close air support strike from an observation post on a hill 1,500 yards east of the town.[13] After directing mortar fire onto German positions in the town, he observed the artillery fire red smoke markers to indicate the targets for the fighter-bombers, that arrived a few minutes later. The first formation circled overhead and dived onto the town from the east, dive bombing and strafing with their machine guns before swinging off to the south and circling back to the east to gain altitude. Then they dived again upon the town, this time strafing only, the process repeated by the following flights. The air attack on Cervaro lasted for half an hour, and assisted the US troops to break into the town, though they still had to use bayonet and grenade to clear the Germans out of their formidable defensive positions in the cellars and amid the rubble. It was an outflanking move to the north by the 1st Special Service Force that finally helped to prise them out of their positions in this sector.

The US 1st Armored Division and the British 46th Division attacked Monte Porchia and the smaller height, Colle Cedro, to the south. In this sector, however, the XIV Panzer Corps forward units received hurried reinforcement by elements of the Hermann Goering Division. The US 6th Armored Infantry were on Monte Porchia by 6 January assisted by fire from supporting tanks, but were pushed back by a counter-attack, and then finally took the hill early on the next day with artillery support, though the attacking battalion was then reduced to 150 men. In the meantime, during the night of 4/5 January, the 138th Infantry Brigade of the British 46th Division attacked across the Peccia to seize Colle Cedro. They met stiff resistance, with the overlooking Monte Porchia being still in German hands, their position became untenable, and they fell back having sustained 250 casualties.

By 10 January, XIV Panzer Corps' own battle casualties since the beginning of the year amounted to 1,506. This represented a steady drain of combat troops and was enough to concern both von Senger and his Army commander, von Vietinghoff, that such a rate would undermine their ability to hold the Gustav Line. The strength of XIV Panzer Corps in mid January was some 90,000 troops, over half of the Tenth Army total of 150,000. Tenth Army, moreover, facing not only Fifth Army but also Eighth Army on the Adriatic sector, could soon become over-stretched. In northern Italy, the Fourteenth Army had a further 70,000 troops, but a sizeable proportion of these were constantly needed to combat Italian partisans and secure communications, and many were still training. Nearer to hand around Rome were some 24,000 troops, but they constituted a reserve against an Allied amphibious landing and so could not be drawn upon lightly. Hauling men out of hospitals and from non-combatant duties might assemble a further 25,000 men,[14] but of very limited effectiveness, and in the harsh conditions of fighting in Italy, such men would be next to useless. Clearly, not only was the pool of effective combat troops finite, but German commanders had always finely to judge the point when the attrition that they were imposing upon the Allies began to work against them. On 13 January XIV Panzer Corps began to abandon Monte Trocchio and Colle Cedro, and pull back into the Gustav Line itself.

Clark's relentless offensive pressure, driven by the 'Shingle' timetable, had obtained positions from which to launch the assault on the Gustav Line. It had been costly. Despite the use of all available artillery, and nearly 1,000 sorties by supporting bombers and fighter-bombers that were airborne whenever the weather allowed, the US casualties alone from 1 to 10 January were nearly 2,000. Yet the troops of Fifth Army had fought through what amounted to only the outposts of the formidable Gustav Line that was now ready and waiting for them.

4

THE FIRST BATTLE OF CASSINO

Nature's Bastion: The Cassino Battlefield

As Fifth Army stood before the Gustav Line, barring its route to Rome along Highway 6 lay not only German defences but also some of the most difficult and forbidding ground ever to confront an army. It was a truly formidable prospect. On its coastal flank, the Rivers Liri, Rapido and Gari joined to become the River Garigliano, flowing southward between rising ground and hills to meet the sea in the Gulf of Gaeta. Overlooking the crossings of the Garigliano were the Aurunci Mountains and, particularly, Monte Majo. To the north of the Liri Valley lay a range of high mountains extending south-west from the Apennines, and running along the valleys of the Rivers Rapido and Milfa. This was a mountain barrier, dominated by the 5,400-foot high Monte Cairo, with the heights of Monte Belvedere and Monte Abate roughly to the north-east. Stretching for five miles to the south of Monte Cairo was a chain of heights running parallel with Highway 6 on its northern side. These were Monte Castellone, then Colle St Angelo and, forming the south-eastern tip of the chain, the 1,700-foot Monte Cassino. Monte Cassino, surmounted by the famous monastery, overlooked the valley of the River Rapido to the east and the River Liri to the south. It dominated Highway 6 as it crossed the Liri just to the south-east, passed through the town of Cassino and then turned south to curve around the base of the mountain before resuming a north-westerly direction.

The Fifth Army Plan

The plan for Fifth Army's offensive against the Gustav Line was dictated by the time imperative, and by the dispositions of its three Corps following the Bernhardt Line fighting, which Clark had little time to alter. His attack would start only ten days before Lucas' VI Corps was due to land at Anzio. As with the earlier attack on the Bernhardt Line, the offensive was sequential in approach. Juin's French Expeditionary Corps, on Fifth Army's right, would begin on 12 January, its 2nd Moroccan and 3rd Algerian Divisions attacking through the mountains towards Atina and San Elia to gain the high ground to the north and north-west of Cassino. They would be followed by Keyes' II Corps, with the US 1st Armored Division and the 34th and 36th Infantry Divisions, attacking to seize Monte Trocchio, the last height before the River Rapido. With the French and Americans closed up to the river, it would fall to McCreery's British X Corps to make the first penetration of the actual Gustav Line. With its 56th and 46th Infantry Divisions, reinforced by the 5th Infantry Division transferred from the Eighth Army sector with great secrecy, and tanks of the 23rd Armoured Brigade, X Corps was to cross the River Garigliano on 17 January. It would seize two bridgeheads, the first near Minturno, on the lower reaches of the Garigliano near its mouth, and the second near the Liri Valley at San Ambrogio, to cover the left flank of II Corps. With the Germans then pinned to the north and south, II Corps in the centre would cross the Rapido at San Angelo. There, to the south of Highway 6 and Cassino, it would establish a bridgehead from which the tanks of 1st Armored Division would break into and through the Liri Valley and advance towards Frosinone, by which time Lucas' VI Corps would have landed at Anzio in the German rear.[1]

Mountain Warfare: The French Expeditionary Corps Reach the Rapido
Opposite Juin's French Corps, the Germans held the heights Costa San Pietro ridge, Monna Casale, Monte Passero, and Monte Monna Acquafondata as an outer defensive ring before the Gustav Line. Beyond, forming part of the Line itself stood the heights Monte Belvedere, Monte Carella, Monte San Croce, and Monte Marrone. Juin's task of capturing these heights was a daunting mountain warfare problem of extremities in both ground and winter weather, but of the troops in Fifth Army, his were the most fitted to tackle it.

In General André Dody's 2nd Moroccan and General Alphonse de Monsabert's 3rd Algerian Divisions, he had extremely hardy North African soldiers of France's *Armée d'Afrique*. These were soldiers well versed in the techniques of mountain warfare, and of moving rapidly on foot in such terrain. They were also trained in, and had a particular aptitude for, the use of infiltration tactics and operating in small units. Each soldier usually carried hard rations for only one or two days, his load being predominantly ammunition and, especially, grenades. They were, however, poorly clothed for the extreme cold and wet, and severe cases of frostbite and 'trench foot' depleted their battalions. They were formidable and enthusiastic fighters, and their French officers and NCOs were

FRENCH EXPEDITIONARY CORPS January – February 1944	PRINCIPAL OPPOSING GERMAN FORMATION **5th Mountain Division** (General Julius Ringel)
2nd Moroccan Division (General André Dody)	
8th Régiment de Tirailleurs Marocains (RTM) 5th RTM, 4th RTM	115th Panzer Grenadier Regiment 85th Mountain Regiment
3rd Algerian Division (General Joseph de Monsabert)	
3rd Régiment de Tirailleurs Algériens (RTA) 7th RTA 4th Régiment de Tirailleurs Tunisiens (RTT)	100th Mountain Regiment
Battalion nomenclature: i.e. 2/8th RTM (2nd Battalion, 8th Régiment de Tirailleurs Marocains)	

highly competent for the battle that confronted them, as well as being determined to restore the military honour of France.

The Moroccans had the task of capturing the Costa San Pietro ridge and the lesser heights to the south, Points 1025 and 1029, and Points 1225 and 1220. They were to assist the Algerian Division to take Monna Casale. The Algerians had also to take Monte Passero and Monte Monna Acquafondata. Late on 11 January, the 8th RTM and 5th Tabour Group crossed the snow-covered slopes of the Mainarde Massif in an outflanking move to take the Costa San Pietro ridge from the north. They succeeded, but then had to hold their positions on the ridge throughout 12 and 13 January against three heavy counter-attacks by the 115th Panzer Grenadier Regiment. The Moroccans had achieved surprise, but the Germans were demonstrating both their characteristic reaction capability, and that the troubles of Allied troops often only began once they were on their objective. This intense fighting saw the forward battalion, the 3/8th RTM, lose three-quarters of its officers and its companies reduced to about 40 men each. Points 1225 and 1220 fell to 4th RTM in a very successful night attack in which the Moroccans closely followed upon the supporting artillery barrage. They caught the German defenders by surprise, killing many of them in their dugouts by throwing in grenades, others they shot down as they ran to man their weapon pits. The Germans had clearly not expected the attackers to reach the heights so quickly after the barrage, but France's North African soldiers would soon be radically revising German opinions of what ground could be traversed, and how quickly.

General de Monsabert gave 7th RTA the task of capturing Monna Casale, but first it had to take two smaller heights that lay in its path, known to the French as the Jumelles. The ground was difficult, steep ridges with bare crests cut by deep ravines, and many of the troops in the attacking battalions were weary, having hauled their own ammunition and supplies forward throughout the day preceding the attack. Early on 12 January, following a barrage, they reached the crests of the Jumelles. Immediate counter-attacks by 3/85th Mountain Regiment pushed them off again, this time the Germans making effective use of their supporting mortars and artillery to inflict heavy casualties upon the Algerian companies strung out on the crests with little cover. For both sides, the ensuing battle for the Jumelles, and for Monna Casale itself, was one of close-quarter fighting by small groups in confusing ground in which grenades and the bayonet were the principal weapons. There was little scope for supporting artillery to intervene in such fighting. Nor could the hundred or so fighter-bombers of XII Air Support Command active over the French front. This was an infantryman's battle, in which the quality of leadership among junior officers and NCOs was decisive, and it was this, perhaps more than any other factor, that secured the eventual French success. Four times the summit of Monna Casale changed hands, but by early on 13 January the Algerian Division held it securely. In the meantime, the Bonjour Group, a battle group composed of a battalion of 4th RTT

THE FIRST BATTLE OF CASSINO

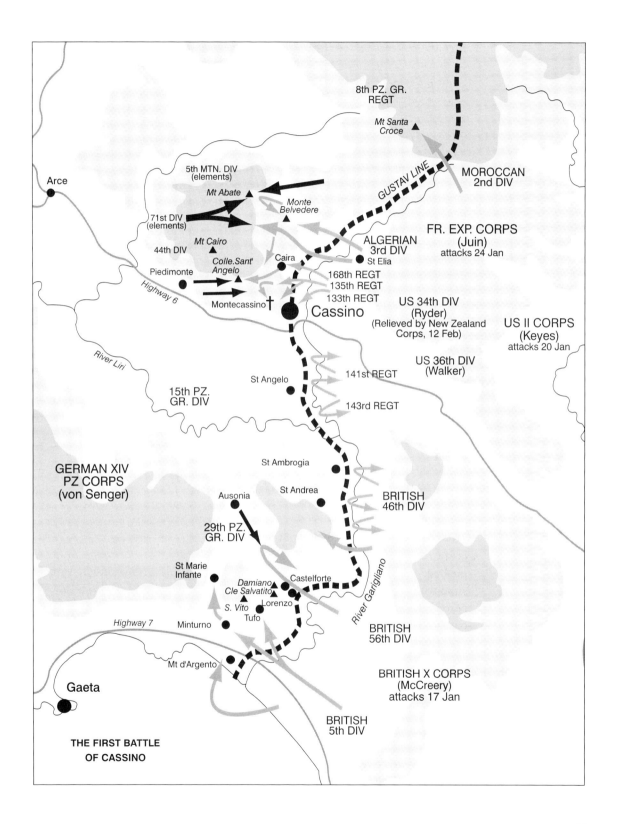

and a squadron from the Division's Reconnaissance Regiment, probed a gap in the German defences near Acquafondata village. This enabled 3rd RTA to change the axis of its advance to capture Monna Acquafondata.

The German 5th Mountain Division began to falter under Juin's pressure. For its mostly young soldiers, actually inexperienced in mountain fighting and inadequately equipped for it, both the cruel weather and the ferocity of the French colonial troops pitted against them proved a severe shock. Casualties were heavy, the battalions reduced to fighting strengths of less than 200, and morale was becoming unsteady. On 13 January, the Divisional Commander, General Ringel, reported to Tenth Army that his losses in some units amounted to 80 per cent, and that his division was being destroyed. That evening Tenth Army sanctioned its partial withdrawal.

As the German line began to give, so Juin pressed harder, the Algerians reaching San Elia and the high ground to the north-east that the Germans had abandoned. The Moroccans were now overlooking the valley of the Rapido and were on the slopes of Monte San Croce. Juin's troops had achieved their objectives, and had advanced four miles over almost impossible terrain in winter, savaging the 5th Mountain Division in the process and causing its withdrawal into the Gustav Line. They were now exhausted, however, and needed respite. This of course was the fundamental problem confronting Clark's Fifth Army. Its attacking formations, their strength quickly reduced by high attrition rates and their survivors weakened by the exertion of winter mountain fighting, were brought to a standstill and left incapable of exploiting their hard-won gains.

BRITISH X CORPS (General Richard McCreery)[2]
For first crossing of the Garigliano

5th Infantry Division (Major-General G Bucknall, Major-General P. Gregson-Ellis after 22 January)
13th Infantry Brigade: 2nd Cameronians, 2nd Royal Inniskilling Fusiliers, 2nd Wiltshire
15th Infantry Brigade: 1st Green Howards, 1st King's Own Yorkshire Light Infantry, 1st Yorks and Lancs
17th Infantry Brigade: 2nd Royal Scots Fusiliers, 2nd Northamptonshire, 6th Seaforth Highlanders
201st Guards Brigade: 6th Grenadier Guards, 3rd Coldstream Guards, 2nd Scots Guards
Artillery support: four field regiments, one medium regiment, one anti-tank regiment.
Amphibious assault craft: 50 DUKWs (53rd QM Battalion, US Army)

56th Infantry Division (Major-General G. Templer)
167th Infantry Brigade: 8th and 9th Royal Fusiliers, 7th Oxfordshire and Buckinghamshire Light Infantry
168th Infantry Brigade: 10th Royal Berkshire, 1st London Scottish, 1st London Irish
169th Infantry Brigade: 2nd/5th, 2nd/6th, 2nd/7th Battalions, The Queen's Royal Regiment
Artillery support: four field regiments, one medium regiment, one anti-tank regiment, plus 2nd AGRA (Army Group Royal Artillery) of one field, three medium, and one heavy regiments, and one field regiment from X Corps.

There were few fresh troops available, and with the breakdown of attack momentum, the Germans gained the reprieve necessary for staged withdrawal to new positions. Nevertheless, Juin's Corps had caused both von Vietinghoff and von Senger considerable worry; both had become increasingly concerned at the threat to XIV Panzer Corps' flank, von Senger later recalling that the battle at times 'seemed to hang by a thread'.[3] In particular, the French Corps seemed capable of penetrating ground thought to be impassable to threaten the rear of German positions. Kesselring shared their concern, and decided to divert 3rd Panzer Grenadier Division, under orders to join LXXVI Panzer Corps opposite Eighth Army, to relieve 5th Mountain Division in von Senger's line. No sooner had he done so, than the XIV Panzer Corps' hitherto quiet sector in the south along the River Garigliano suddenly and unexpectedly burst into flames.

British X Corps Crosses the Garigliano

This was the coastal sector, where the Germans had to guard against seaborne landings as well as frontal attack, and their troops were thin on the ground. Responsible for this sector was the 94th Infantry Division, a '1944-type' division with only two battalions in each of its three regiments. It was inexperienced, its reliability untested and doubted by both von Vietinghoff and von Senger. Its 274th Grenadier Regiment held positions from the coast to the valley of the south-flowing River Ausente, including the heights around Minturno, while the 276th Grenadier Regiment covered the Castelforte area. Further back, the 267th Regiment was watching the coast. In support was a tank battalion of the Hermann Goering Panzer Division. The 94th Division had few outposts on the east bank of the Garigliano. Its strongest positions, with interlocking fields of fire for mortars and machine-guns, were in the wooded hills running from the coast inland to the Castelforte area and overlooking the likely crossings on the Garigliano. The sowing of at least 24,000 mines compensated to an extent for a lack of troops.

Although McCreery held an advantage of three to one in divisions, the X Corps' task was formidable, and fighting in Italy was never simply a matter of numbers. With the Highway 7 road bridge and the railway bridge over the river both demolished by the Germans, and the water too deep to ford, the crossing would have to be by assault boats. These were in short supply, and there would be a shortage of DUKW amphibious vehicles in Fifth Army following the only rehearsal for the 'Shingle' seaborne landings during which many were lost at sea.[4] Once across the river, there would be very few roads and tracks leading into the high ground suitable for vehicles, so the momentum of X Corps' attack and much of the forward supply would depend upon foot movement and mules. Of the latter, there were not enough, only just over 1,000 for the whole Corps, and in the high ground the infantry, once again, would have to act as porters. For many, this would mean strenuous climbing, often for hours at a time, while hauling food, water and ammunition by hand. Casualty evacuation would mean a similar nightmare in reverse to reach the nearest point accessible to vehicles.

In view of the scale of its task, and that so much would depend on the infantry battalions, X Corps would be fully stretched even with 5th Division, and McCreery's only reserve was a single Commando brigade.

McCreery intended that the 5th and 56th Divisions make the initial crossing over the Garigliano and carve out a bridgehead some four miles deep and eight miles wide. Then, 5th Division would push out units a further ten miles towards San Giorgio to secure an opening into the Liri Valley leading to Pontecorvo. The second crossing to the north-east near San Ambrogio on US II Corps' flank would be the task of 46th Division. While the decision to employ two divisions to establish a secure bridgehead appears logical, it undermined the emphasis of Clark's plan, which was to support II Corps. It was a question of priorities, because McCreery did not have the requisite force to carry out both tasks in strength. However, his decision to allocate only one division to the San Ambrogio crossing, and its timing, implied a lack of commitment to supporting II Corps. The American reaction was one of dismay. Keyes also expected the British to cross forty-eight hours before his own crossing of the Rapido, to enable them to capture the ridge above San Ambrogio, thereby denying the Germans observation over the low ground of the American crossing. Shortly before the start of the X Corps attack, Keyes learnt that the 46th Division's crossing had been postponed and would occur only twenty-four hours ahead of his own, and that the high ground was not among its objectives. Blaming a 'British unwillingness to launch attacks in force',[5] he requested a postponement of the II Corps crossing, arguing that unless the 46th Division provided full support, his own effort would likely fail. Clark, driven by the 'Shingle' timetable, refused.

River Crossing: The 5th Division
During the night of 15/16 January 5th Division occupied its jumping-off positions in the coastal sector on the left of X Corps' front. Some 45 assault boats and numerous rafts were collected, at distances no further than 2,000 yards inland of the river bank. Gun positions were already dug and camouflaged and artillery ammunition dumped, but there was to be no artillery barrage preceding the crossing. The 5th Division was going in silent, to achieve surprise, and the troops in the leading battalions, their equipment padded, were ordered to display no lights and make no noise. Spearheading the attack was 13th Brigade on the right, crossing the river near Minturno, and 17th Brigade on the left between Minturno and the coast.

On the coastal flank there was also an amphibious element. The 2nd Royal Scots Fusiliers in US-manned DUKW amphibious vehicles, with some supporting tanks and self-propelled artillery in landing-craft, were to go ashore some 2,000 yards behind the German lines on the west bank of the river estuary. The objective of the first wave, A and B Companies, was Monte d'Argento, a height from which the Germans could enfilade the coastal reaches of the Garigliano. Then C and D companies, also in DUKWs, were to pass through towards

Minturno to clear two smaller heights and support the river crossing. Fire support from the sea included the guns of two cruisers and five destroyers of the Royal Navy standing off the coast. They were ready to suppress German fire from the hills inland, and to harass the roads through which German reinforcements must pass. From the air, light bombers, and the fighter-bombers of the US XII Air Support Command, prepared to isolate the bridgehead by interdicting German movement; they would also attack German positions and artillery during the bridgehead battle.

On 5th Division's front the night amphibious assault went awry from the start. An advance party to set up guiding lights for the DUKWs landed too late to prevent confusion, an enemy to amphibious operations every bit as dangerous as the Germans. To begin with, the DUKWs had to make an eleven-mile sea journey along the coast from Mondragone, an ambitious distance for such craft to navigate, and beyond the experience of their crews. Many became lost.[6] Only A Company and a few others of the Fusiliers landed correctly on the north bank of the estuary, the remainder, including the Beach Command Group, landed on the south bank behind 5th Division's lines. Unaware of this, some of these troops were about to attack their own Brigade headquarters, though this catastrophe was prevented in time. During the run-in, the phosphorescence of the sea enabled German spotters to see the craft, surprise was lost and soon accurate German shellfire came down. Once ashore, many of the troops found their weapons clogged by damp sand, and the increasing confusion denied them heavier support. Observing no guiding lights ashore, the landing-craft bringing the supporting tanks and anti-tank guns waited, but eventually returned to Mondragone with their cargoes.

It took time to sort out the confusion in the river mouth, but when the Fusiliers set off to attack d'Argento they found themselves in a huge minefield swept by mortar and small-arms fire, and pinned down. There were only two mine detectors in the battalion, and no sappers to assist; they were in the landing-craft that had turned back. By dawn, 5th Division's artillery was providing fire support, but d'Argento did not fall until later in the day following a German withdrawal. The amphibious assault, in which nothing had gone according to plan, cost 2nd Royal Scots Fusiliers 140 casualties, and the 5th Division's schedule was completely out. There was no chance of a coordinated advance on Minturno by 17th Brigade during the morning of 18 January as intended, not least because the river crossings of the other two battalions had also run into trouble.

The initial problem was mines which the Germans had sown extensively along both banks, and they caused heavy casualties to 2nd Northamptonshires and 6th Seaforth Highlanders. Tapes put up hastily by the battalions were not enough to prevent men stepping on the thickly sown anti-personnel mines, to be killed outright or to lose limbs. By dawn on 18 January both battalions were across the river, but fighting desperately to beat off counter-attacks by 94th Divi-

THE FIRST BATTLE OF CASSINO

sion supported by tanks of the Hermann Goering Panzer Regiment. The 6th Seaforths, near the road just south of Minturno, were particularly hard pressed and had one company overrun. Only the arrival of a forward artillery observer averted disaster; he directed the fire of five field regiments onto the German tanks and they quickly withdrew. This type of responsive and accurate fire support was crucial, and the successful establishment of a bridgehead would depend upon it. The 17th Brigade was pinned, however, and the 5th Division's commander decided to feed in 15th Brigade, originally held back for exploitation towards Ausonia. As its alerted battalions moved forward they too had casualties to mines. Only later when German maps were captured was the full extent of these minefields realised; 5th Division aptly described the whole coastal belt as a 'mine marsh'.

On 17th Brigade's right, 5th Division's other assaulting Brigade, the 13th, also suffered from confusion. The 2nd Wiltshires were across the river by midnight.

Below: Keeping troops supplied in the mountains depended upon mules, and there were never enough of them. This supply column is moving up towards Monte Majo to help sustain Juin's French Expeditionary Corps.

Some 1,300 yards away on their right, the 2nd Royal Inniskilling Fusiliers reached the river to find only a few boats, enough for the leading platoon only, as most had been carried forward to the wrong place. With surprise now lost and his troops under mortar and shellfire, the battalion commander hurried over to the Wiltshires' crossing to arrange for his men to use their boats. By 0300 the Inniskillings were across the river, and fighting hard against strongpoints, particularly a group of farm buildings at Massa Rossi. 'A' Company, which came under heavy mortar fire, attacked these, but soon all its officers were casualties, and by the time the strongpoint was cleared the Company had been reduced to twenty men. That clearing a single strongpoint could see a company cut down to less than a platoon shows how rapid the expenditure of the infantry cutting edge in attack could be, and the crucial importance of fire support. In their attack upon Point 156, a height to the east of Tufo, the Inniskillings were able to follow closely upon their artillery barrage and quickly clear their objective, capturing many of the German defenders still sheltering in their dugouts. By evening, however, a German counter-attack had forced them back off the crest. The Wiltshires cleared Tufo village in house-to-house fighting, but German counter-attacks prevented them securing the overlooking San Vito Ridge. With the British troops only just across the river and precariously established, it was the supporting artillery that prevented these initial counter-attacks from succeeding. The 5th Division's history acknowledges that in this period, it was the Gunners who held the small bridgehead, the Divisional artillery firing unceasingly.[7]

River Crossing: The 56th Division
On the X Corps' right, the 56th Division, with some 72 assault boats and additional rafts, prepared to cross. Among its objectives were the Damiano heights and Monte Rotundo to the west of Castelforte. Unlike 5th Division, the 56th's crossing was preceded by a heavy artillery barrage and counter-battery fire against German gun positions, for which extra artillery was allotted. Despite this support, their crossing encountered similar problems to that of 5th Division, and also had its share of confusion. Crossing on the right, the 169th (Queen's) Brigade's assault battalions, 2/6th and 2/5th Queen's, first faced the strain of carrying their boats a considerable distance and crossing an irrigation ditch before reaching the river itself. The 2/6th crossed successfully, but mortar concentrations disrupted the crossing of the 2/5th further upstream and sank several boats; the battalion was across by dawn but had sustained heavy casualties. During 18 January the 2/7th crossed the river and took Sujo village, while the 2/6th and 2/5th established themselves on the high ground to the east. The 167th Brigade on the left crossed opposite the strongly fortified sector embracing Lorenzo and Castelforte and overlooked by Salvatito and, further beyond, Monte Damiano. Once across the river near Scafa Orve and reaching the railway embankment, 9th Royal Fusiliers met determined opposition. 'D' Company sustained heavy casualties, including its commander, and the Battalion's Head-

quarters group, moving in the wrong direction along the embankment, ran into the sights of a machine-gun position. Wireless communication broke down, and both the Adjutant and the Battalion Commander were out of contact; the latter was encountered, bleeding from the mouth and looking for his headquarters, by machine-gunners of the 6th Cheshires moving up in support.[8] An ever-present risk in battle is the extent to which confusion and disorganisation can take hold and spread, and in this instance they were causing the breakdown of attack momentum as surely as the German fire.

The crossings of 8th Royal Fusiliers and 7th Ox and Bucks had better luck, and both battalions made sufficient progress to ease the pressure on 9th Royal Fusiliers. The Ox and Bucks captured Lorenzo, while 8th Royal Fusiliers reached the spur beneath the summit of Monte Damiano. This was punishing work, a climb of some 1,300 feet up a terraced hillside with, at intervals, six-foot retaining walls. By the end of the day, the reorganised 9th Royal Fusiliers had secured Colle Salvatito.

Although it had fallen short of its intended timetable and initial objectives, by the end of 18 January X Corps was across the Garigliano. Its ability to stay there depended upon reinforcing and supplying the bridgehead as quickly as possible, which in turn depended upon bridges. This amounted to a race, to build the necessary bridges and strengthen the bridgehead before the Germans could amass sufficient troops and armour for a major counter-attack. In 5th Division's sector, engineers had four large cable-hauled rafts working, and behind 56th Division a pontoon raft-ferry. The Germans were well aware of their importance, and their mortar and artillery fire, directed by observers on the high ground overlooking the river, successfully disrupted attempts to construct larger bridges for vehicles and armour. Early on 19 January, engineers completed a folding boat bridge, but the first vehicle across exploded an undetected mine. This took three hours to clear, but damage from shellfire later in the day closed the bridge for nine hours. The German gunners also sank several heavy rafts; fortunately for X Corps, they had comparatively few guns and limited ammunition. Throughout daylight on 18 and 19 January US Kittyhawk and Mustang fighter-bombers were also out in strength over the Garigliano battle area, helping to suppress German fire and harassing their movement.

The Germans: Riposte

Although the German Tenth Army Headquarters was unable to read the battle sufficiently to determine Fifth Army's intentions when reporting the X Corps attack to Kesselring early on 18 January, Kesselring was in no doubt at all. This was part of a major offensive to break the Gustav Line south of Cassino and he was determined to defeat it. He decided to reinforce von Senger, who telephoned his concern to him direct from the 94th Division's command post to request the release of the reserves held back in the event of an Allied seaborne landing.[9] The remote possibility of such a landing did not concern Kesselring's local commanders half so much as the 94th Division's crumbling front, and von

Senger certainly was in no doubt about the serious threat posed by the British crossing. First, Kesselring ordered all the uncommitted units of 94th Division, including cooks and drivers, into the battle to reinforce the local counter-attacks already under way. Then he earmarked three battalions of the 15th Panzer Grenadier Division and the 2nd Hermann Goering Panzer Grenadier Regiment as immediate reserves. He also identified further reinforcements for XIV Panzer Corps' southern flank; the 134th Grenadier Regiment of the 44th Infantry Division, and the reconnaissance battalions of the 3rd Panzer Grenadier and 44th and 71st Infantry Divisions. He halted the relief of 5th Mountain Division, opposite the French, by 3rd Panzer Grenadier Division, and sent the latter's artillery, along with batteries of medium guns from LXXVI Panzer Corps, to the Garigliano. True to form, Kesselring was reacting quickly, but then the Tenth Army staff became seriously concerned, as did Kesselring, that the Allies were about to launch an attack in the San Angelo–Cassino area with some five divisions. What had worried them, and induced this belief, was the British 46th Division.

River Crossing Failure: 46th Division
On the evening of 19 January, the 46th Division attempted to cross the Garigliano near San Ambrogio, and failed. The task was entrusted to the 128th (Hampshire) Brigade. The Hampshires were to seize the initial bridgehead including the village and a low ridge to the north and south. Then, the 138th Brigade were to cross and exploit westward to conform with the intended northward advance of 5th and 56th Divisions. A thick fog over the river and no German activity boded well for the crossing, but the river itself did not. It was flowing far too fast; the Germans had opened the sluices of an irrigation dam farther to the north, swelling the river and forcing a strong current. At the 5th Hampshires' crossing on the left, a single assault boat reached the opposite bank with a cable, but this soon snapped as they tried to haul more boats over, and further attempts only saw the boats swept down-river. The 1st/4th Hampshires met the same difficulties; repeated attempts to get a cable across by boat and by the plucky efforts of the strongest swimmers were all defeated by the current.

Crossing on the right, the boats carrying the first company of 2nd Hampshires were swept along by the current to crash against the opposite bank downstream. These troops were at least across the river, but what boats remained unbroken could not possibly make the return journey against the current to fetch reinforcements. They were isolated, and then the Germans holding the sector, a battalion of the 15th Panzer Grenadier Division's 129th Panzer Grenadier Regiment, woke up to what was happening on the river and began to react. Only a few of the 2nd Hampshires' company returned across the river, and early on 20 January, with German resistance and artillery fire increasing, General Hawkesworth of 46th Division called a halt. There were no further attempts by 46th Division to cross in this area. The 128th Brigade remained in place and 138th Brigade was moved immediately to reinforce the 56th Division's bridgehead where, admittedly, more infantry were needed.

Keyes' II Corps viewed the 46th Division's effort as half-hearted and an example of excessive British caution and a failure to persevere, and it caused some bitterness.[10] General Frederick Walker's US 36th Infantry Division preparing to cross the Rapido, five miles to the north at San Angelo, would now have its left flank completely unprotected. Despite his own consternation at the 46th's failure, and McCreery now urging him to cancel the 36th Division's attempt, Clark held to his plan. He was determined to open the Liri Valley, and determined to draw the maximum number of German forces away from the 'Shingle' landing area. On 20 January, he decided that, even at the risk of heavy casualties, the 36th Division would cross the Rapido at San Angelo.

River Crossing Débâcle: The US 36th Division

The US 36th Division was to cross the Rapido on either side of the village of San Angelo and establish a bridgehead extending to Pignataro, some two miles distant, from which Combat Command 'B' of 1st Armored Division, three tank battalions and a regiment of Armored Infantry, were to exploit into the Liri Valley. Irrespective of the failure of the British 46th Division, the odds were already stacked heavily against the 36th Division ever getting across the river, let alone establishing a firm bridgehead. The widths of the Rapido in that sector varied from twenty-five to fifty feet, and it was vertically banked each side to between three and six feet. The river was fast-flowing, and up to twelve feet deep. The Germans had flooded the low-lying eastern bank, turning the ground over which the American troops had to approach the river into a marsh that they had also extensively mined. There was no cover, and these approaches were under observation from German positions on the western side, and covered by their mortars and artillery. Immediately overlooking the river was the village of San Angelo, stepped up on a forty-foot rise. More distant but dominating the river valley, and of which none of the American troops could be unaware, was German-occupied Monte Cassino and the great monastery.

For those seeing it for the first time, the sight of the huge building high on top of the mountain was a surprise, and very awesome. 'Like a lion it crouched,' recalled American veteran Harold L. Bond of his first view of the monastery as a young lieutenant in January 1944, 'dominating all approaches, watching every move made by the armies down below'.[11]

General Walker was deeply unhappy about his division's attack, fatalistically recording his doubts about its success to his diary in a manner similar to that of Lucas' about 'Shingle'. Whereas Lucas, for good or ill, would have at least some control over events at Anzio, at the Rapido Walker had none. His division was to attack, and he felt sure that it was about to be sacrificed. Night patrols probing across the river provided some indications of the German defences, and of the presence of mines and barbed wire, but not their truly formidable strength. In fact, the 36th Division was preparing to enter an inferno. The 3rd/104th Panzer Grenadier Regiment and the 1st/129th Panzer Grenadier Regiment held the San Angelo area, both belonging to the 15th Panzer Grenadier Division, with the 3rd Panzer Battalion of the Hermann Goering Panzer Division in support. The German positions were extensive. Shell-battered San Angelo provided excellent cover for machine-guns and mortars, and there was a linked belt of dugouts and slit trenches. These, sited between 200 to 1,000 yards from the river, had good fields of fire. German troops also patrolled aggressively on the western bank, interfering with American engineers attempting to reconnoitre for suitable crossing sites and trying to clear mines and tape out approach routes. The Germans must have known by such evidence that a crossing was in preparation, though perhaps not its importance, and the 36th Division did not seriously challenge their patrol domination of both banks in the days before the attempt.

Walker intended to make the crossing in darkness late on 20 January with two infantry regiments. The 141st to the north of San Angelo would send its 1st Battalion across in assault boats, while the 3rd would follow in boats and on footbridges erected by engineers. To the south of San Angelo the 1st and 3rd Battalions of the 143rd Infantry would cross simultaneously, their first wave in assault boats, the rest on foot bridges. In daylight, smoke generators would mask the crossing sites from observation. Artillery support consisted of sixteen battalions of field artillery, ready to bombard the German positions for thirty minutes before the crossing and thereafter to provide observed fire support. During daylight on 20 January, P-40 Kittyhawk and A-20 fighter-bombers of the XII Air Support Command also made 124 sorties, bombing suspected strongpoints in San Angelo, and attacking German movement and gun positions near Cassino.

Within the 36th Division there were problems that further undermined its already slim chance of success. Morale was fragile. The Division had suffered heavily during the Bernhardt Line fighting, each of its regiments being depleted by nearly a thousand men. Replacements arriving in early January only made up for about half of these losses and the new men were inexperienced and new to their units, with little time to become assimilated as members of a team. Partly due to the turnover in personnel and partly due to the limited time for preparation, there was poor staff work for a river-crossing operation. There was little coordination and planning between the infantry and the engineers whose skills and capabilities were essential. These internal problems might have been eliminated had the Division received a period of rest and reorganisation, but this was not possible. Instead, it confronted a task that has become known as one of the most notorious forlorn hopes of military history. Throughout the Division there was an awareness of the immense difficulty of their task, and of the likely prospect awaiting them at the river. Even the best soldiers are only human and feel that if they are deliberately committed to an attack they ought at least to have some chance. The 36th Division knew that it had very little, and anxiety and pessimism are not the preserve of Divisional commanders.

At 1930 on 20 January, in dense fog, the American guns began to fire their preparation, and 36th Division's assault battalions began to move forward; most troops carried an extra belt of ammunition and bayonets were fixed. Accurate German artillery and mortar fire immediately began to fall on the approaches, smashing many of the dumped assault boats and causing heavy casualties among the troops struggling to carry other boats and bridging material forward over the long approach to the river bank. Many men under fire strayed into the minefields, causing further casualties; many dropped and abandoned their boats, and confusion grew. At the 1st/141st Infantry's crossing, at least a quarter of the engineers' equipment was destroyed. They erected four floating-duckboard foot bridges, all of which were soon damaged, and eventually only one, sufficiently intact to allow individuals to cross carefully one at a time, remained in place. By dawn on 21 January only about a hundred troops at most were across, out of contact with the eastern bank as all radios were lost and lines cut. The Assistant Divisional Commander, General Wilbur, postponed the crossing of the 3rd/141st as too hazardous in daylight, sending a messenger across to the far bank to tell the troops to dig in and await reinforcement. The 1st/143rd experienced similar difficulties, but by dawn was across the river. Moving against the German positions proved impossible; the troops were pinned under heavy fire once daylight revealed their positions, and several German tanks began to close in. Lacking anti-tank weapons and in danger of annihilation, such troops as could return were withdrawn to the eastern bank. The 3rd/143rd attempt completely broke down under heavy fire and confusion, and no troops crossed the river.

Early on the morning of January 21, Clark received intelligence reports of German reinforcements moving south towards the Garigliano–Rapido sectors and, as the Allies had hoped, away from the Anzio area. He contacted Keyes and directed him to get tanks and tank-destroyers across the Rapido as soon as possible. With 'Shingle' due to take place on the following day, it was imperative to reach the Liri Valley. Keyes, visiting Walker's headquarters later that morning, found the situation at the Rapido and learned that Walker was preparing a renewed crossing attempt for that evening. Keyes insisted on an immediate effort, though with the prevailing disorganisation and confusion at the river it was late afternoon before the 3rd/143rd were ready. They crossed under cover of smoke, using all the boats that could be scraped together, followed by companies of the 2nd and 1st Battalions. Once across, they tried to advance but five hundred yards from the bank intense fire halted them. Not even the greatest courage could get the attack moving, though Staff Sergeant Thomas McCall of the 2nd/143rd, leading his company against German emplacements, earned a posthumous Medal of Honor in the attempt. The American artillery could help little, the smoke and a lack of pre-registered targets frustrated its observers, and radio and telephone communication with the troops across the river was lost. It proved impossible for the engineers to erect Bailey bridges suitable for armour or to bring forward the necessary equipment to do so, and only footbridges under enemy fire remained. Later in the evening, to the north of San Angelo, the 2nd/141st crossed the river, followed by the 3rd Battalion crossing on footbridges. They found no survivors from the 1st Battalion, and German fire stopped their own attack with heavy casualties about 1,000 yards beyond the river, where they dug-in.

During 22 January, the situation of the American troops in their narrow bridgeheads across the river became hopeless. Casualties were mounting under the increasing fire and counter-attack, and ammunition was running out. In the early afternoon most of the 143rd Infantry were withdrawn to the near bank. The battalions of the 141st were less fortunate. With their footbridges destroyed under German fire they were isolated, and only small parties returned by swimming across the river. During the evening, the 36th Division's troops on the near bank, powerless to assist their trapped comrades over the river, listened to their gunfire as they fought on to hold their positions. Eventually the sound of American weapons died away.

The 36th Division's crossing attempt was over, and it had cost 1,681 casualties: 143 killed, 663 wounded, and 875 missing. At first the Germans could make little sense of this battle. The commander of the 15th Panzer Grenadier Division, General Rodt, reported to XIV Panzer Corps that his troops had successfully repelled a crossing attempt, and that it had not been necessary to draw upon reserves. His own losses had been 64 killed and 179 wounded. Only when the full extent of the American dead and the number of prisoners, some 500, became known did von Senger and his XIV Panzer Corps staff realise what the 36th Division had attempted, and the extent of their own defensive success.[12]

'Shingle': The German Intelligence Picture Changes

In mid-January, although Kesselring was well aware of the possibility of a Fifth Army offensive against the Gustav Line, and of an Allied seaborne landing on his flank, he expected neither imminently. When, following the French attack against XIV Panzer Corps' left, the British X Corps attack opened on its right along the Garigliano, Kesselring was immediately under pressure from his local commanders to release his reserves. The 94th Division in the coastal sector was likely to be overwhelmed, and both von Vietinghoff and von Senger were clamouring for reinforcement with which to counter-attack. Kesselring yielded, somewhat against his own better judgement, but he realised that if Tenth Army's right wing collapsed, the restoring of a defensive line might prove impossible. It was an awkward dilemma, and Kesselring could not be sure that he was reading the battle correctly.[13] To the British Ultra code-breakers intercepting the consequent flurry of German signals, Kesselring was demonstrating his brisk decisiveness as a theatre commander, but by 22 January they had confirmation of what they were waiting for. The Headquarters of the I Parachute Corps had been sent from Rome to the Garigliano. Its orders were to take over not only the 94th Divi-

THE FIRST BATTLE OF CASSINO

sion already there, but also the 29th and 90th Panzer Grenadier Divisions that had been recuperating out of the line near the capital.[14] Kesselring had taken the bait, and received the endorsement of Hitler who ordered the Gustav Line to be held at all costs. British X Corps had, like a magnet, drawn south the reserves Kesselring had held back to repel a seaborne landing, and the way for 'Shingle' was clear.

Early on 22 January, Lucas' VI Corps landed unopposed at Anzio. There was only a company of German troops in the small town, and they were soon rounded up, but their report of the landing caused surprise and consternation throughout the German command. Kesselring was caught with his guard down, his reserves committed to the battle along the Garigliano and he knew that he had nothing between Anzio and the Alban Hills and Rome. The German army of the Second World War was never off balance for long, however, and Kesselring,

Below: The gateway to Rome: the Liri Valley with Highway 6 running along the far side of the valley under the mountains. The lower spur in the left middle ground is Monte Cassino surmounted by the ruins of the monastery, and the high ground in the left background is Monte Cairo. This photograph depicts the harsh mountainous terrain encountered in Italy, and the obvious importance of the Liri Valley to mechanised armies.

believing that he was racing against time, reacted at once. He expected the Allied landing force to advance immediately on Rome and cut XIV Panzer Corps' lines of communication. So did von Senger who on hearing of the landing suggested an immediate withdrawal of his right wing in order to conserve his troops and free reserves. Later, von Vietinghoff also suggested a withdrawal from the Gustav Line. Having previously paid little attention to the risk of an Allied seaborne landing, whereas Kesselring always had, von Senger and von Vietinghoff now became extremely and understandably nervous at the thought of an Allied landing force to their rear. Indeed, their reactions go some way to vindicate the hope held by Churchill and Alexander that 'Shingle' would alarm the Germans out of the Gustav Line. Kesselring would have none of it. He refused to panic, particularly as throughout the day the Allied landing force at Anzio made no significant aggressive move. Instead, he ordered von Senger on to the defensive. He allowed

EXAMPLES OF BRITISH BATTALION CASUALTIES (X Corps) Garigliano Battle 18–30 January 1944[15]	
2nd Wiltshires	195
2/7th Queen's	195
1st Green Howards	128
7th Ox & Bucks Light Infantry	180
1st King's Own Yorkshire Light Infantry	174
1st York and Lancaster	253
2nd Royal Scots Fusiliers	193
8th Royal Fusiliers	144
10th Royal Berkshire	136
Total X Corps battle casualties, 23 January to 13 February 1944: 4,145	

him to keep the 29th Panzer Grenadiers, but directed him to send north units of the 15th Panzer Grenadier and Hermann Goering Panzer Divisions and most of 3rd Panzer Grenadier Division. Fourteenth Army in northern Italy was alerted to send units to Anzio immediately.

On 22 January, as Walker's 36th Division fought to cross the Rapido, Lucas' troops that had moved inland from the sea stared at the empty roads before them, and wondered why their orders were to halt and dig-in. Already, by that evening, a thin screen of troops and anti-tank guns of various German units rushed to the area ringed the beachhead. For the next two days these troops anxiously watched the British and Americans, who appeared to be only pushing forward reconnaissance teams and patrols. Two days later, the Germans were no longer worried that the Allies would break out towards Rome. Their own units ringing the beachhead, now seven miles deep and sixteen miles long, were strongly reinforced. Moving mainly at night to avoid Allied air attack, the Germans had reacted with astonishing speed, and more troops were also on the way. The OKW had activated Plan Marder I, the reinforcement of Kesselring by designated formations, including divisions from France and the Balkans, in the event of a major Allied amphibious landing on the Italian west coast.

As early as January 23, Kesselring ordered von Mackensen of Fourteenth Army to strengthen the ring around Anzio, and to begin reducing the beachhead. If Lucas ever had an opportunity to reach the Alban Hills and Rome, it was now gone and the Allies would have to fight hard to break out. That, however, would not be their problem for some time. Instead, they would have to defend their beachhead against the determination of Hitler and Kesselring to drive them back into the sea. Kesselring, while remaining on the defensive along the Gustav Line, was about to take the offensive in Italy against the Allies at Anzio. This would compel Alexander to maintain his own offensive against the Gustav Line in order to ease the pressure against the beachhead, where he would be fighting a major defensive battle – an unforeseen and ironic consequence of 'Shingle'.

Mountain Warfare: Attrition on the Garigliano

From 20 January to 9 February the British X Corps faced a severe battle in the Garigliano bridgehead. The arrival in the Garigliano sector of the 29th and 90th Panzer Grenadier Divisions, following Kesselring's decision to commit his reserves against the X Corps' bridgehead, saw heavy German counter-attacks in the areas Colle Salvatito, Monte Damiano and Tufo. These attacks, pressed home in some cases with reckless courage, were repulsed only by the stubborn determination of the British troops to hold the ground they had gained. Once again, the scale and quality of their supporting firepower proved decisive; on 22 January, with the German attacks at their height, the artillery supporting 56th Division fired almost non-stop for five hours.[16] Late that day, following the news of the Allied landing at Anzio, the Germans went over to the defensive, having regained Monte Natale, commanding the initial stretch of the road between Minturno and Ausonia, and the crest of Monte Damiano.

With the 5th, 56th and 46th Divisions concentrated in the bridgehead, McCreery now resumed his offensive on the axis Castelforte–Ausonia. In the ensuing fighting, the British troops confronted a series of rugged heights, averaging 2,000 feet, divided by steep valleys. Initial attempts by 17th Brigade to recapture Monte Natale with 6th Seaforths and 2nd Royal Scots Fusiliers, and by 168th Brigade to take the crest of Damiano with the 1st London Scottish and 10th Royal Berkshires failed despite considerable determination and bravery. This was the inevitable small-unit fighting, in which men capable of motivating others by example came to the fore, such as Private G. A. Mitchell of the London Scottish, who earned a posthumous Victoria Cross by leading attacks on four German positions.[17] In such fighting, however, the greatest bravery was often not enough to overcome strong defensive zones consisting of small but well-protected and mutually supporting positions, difficult to locate and neutralise with fire, yet dominating the slopes and ridges with their machine-guns and mortars. The British troops had to deal with these positions one by one, closing in to use grenades, automatic weapons and often ultimately the bayonet. Attack momentum could quickly break down in this difficult ground over which few troops could go forward at a time, and where they could be easily pinned by defensive fire. It was slow, laborious and costly work, of the type only the infantry could do.

The 138th Brigade of 46th Division, in a move intended to outflank Castelforte, traversed difficult ground, their ammunition and supplies hauled by mules and by hand. Their objectives, Monte Rotundo East, Monte Furlito and Monte Purgatorio, were held by three battalions of the 94th Infantry and 29th Panzer Grenadier Divisions. By 30 January, these objectives were taken, and in some instances the attacking British troops achieved surprise, indicating their increasing proficiency in mountain fighting. By then Monte Natale was also finally captured. Castelforte and the crest of Monte Damiano remained in German hands, however, when in early February, through a combination of exhaustion and the need to send troops to reinforce the Anzio beachhead, X Corps went over to the defensive. There could be no further progress in this sector, and during the fortnight of intensive fighting since the crossing of the Garigliano X Corps' cutting edge, its battalion rifle companies, had been considerably blunted by heavy casualties.

Resuming the Offensive

At the main Fifth Army front on 23 January, Clark impressed upon his corps commanders the urgency of breaking through the Gustav Line to the Liri Valley and of a rapid link-up with the Anzio beachhead. The impossibility of immediately renewing a frontal assault following the failure of the British 46th and US 36th Divisions, and with X Corps fully engaged along the Garigliano, left few options. Yet Alexander and Clark knew that they had dealt the Germans some heavy blows, and although so far these had been insufficient, they believed that by maintaining their offensive pressure the Gustav Line must crack. Moreover, with Lucas now ashore at Anzio, and German strength building up around his beachhead, they had little choice. Clark turned now to the high ground north of Cassino as the route through which to envelop the German defences barring the entrance to the Liri Valley. The task fell to Keyes, who had General Ryder's 34th Infantry Division so far uncommitted at the Rapido, and Juin, whose French Corps had just resumed its attack in the direction of Atina. Now, the 34th was to cross the Rapido north of Cassino, where it could be forded, and make one thrust south along the river to capture the town. Another thrust would carry the heights overlooking Cassino, including Monte Castellone and Colle San Angelo, the Albaneta Farm and Piedimonte, to break into the Liri Valley some four miles behind Cassino. Juin was now to change the axis of his attack to the south-west, directing his thrust towards Terrelle and Piedimonte, thereby threatening XIV Panzer Corps' lines of communication. In view of the time imperative imposed upon both Clark and Alexander by 'Shingle', and as an immediate line of attack through which to deal XIV Panzer Corps a further blow and possibly dislodge it from its positions, the concept was sound enough. It was asking a great deal, however, of very limited forces, and for the American, French and North African soldiers it would be agony.

France on Belvedere: Juin's Attack

To conform to his changed axis of attack Juin had to move the 3rd Algerian Division, no easy task during the course of a battle, and adjust his Corps' supply points. Nevertheless, on 25 January the 3rd Algerian began its battle to secure Monte Belvedere and Monte Abate, in some of the hardest mountain fighting of the Italian campaign. Monte Belvedere was an attacker's nightmare, consisting of a series of summits; Points 862, 681, 721 and 771. Another, Point 700, lay a mile to the west overlooking the road to Terrelle, and a mile further north was Monte Abate consisting of Points 875 and 915. This high ground constituted a formidable barrier to the Liri Valley, and was held by three German battalions of the 44th and 71st Infantry Divisions. The Algerian Division approached over the hills west of the Rapido, forded the river Secco waist-deep, then moved westward up the slopes along two routes. One was a thousand-foot ascent along a steep gully, later known as 'Gandoët Gully' in honour of Major Gandoët, commander of the 3rd Battalion of the 4th Tunisian Infantry. The other was a steep climb from Point

382 leading to Points 700 and 771. This was no terrain over which an attacker might be expected to move, and that was precisely why the French chose it. There was a chance of surprise, and of avoiding the strongest German positions covering the Rapido valley, and they knew that their troops were among the few that would be capable of fighting after the tremendous exertion of the ascent.

From 25 to 31 January the battalions of the 3rd Algerian Division's 4th Tunisian Infantry secured Monte Belvedere and Monte Abate. The fighting involved a series of attacks and counter-attacks, the reduction of German bunker positions one by one, and the holding of ground, once taken, against desperate attempts to retake it. For the Germans were desperate; von Senger well realised the threat posed from the north to the Cassino position, and with Kesselring's support every available man was committed. Eventually some six battalions, supported by artillery and mortars, an assault gun battery and three troops of *Nebelwerfer* six-barrelled rocket projectors, were employed in an attempt to stem the French attack and throw it back. On occasions when these counter-attacks succeeded in regaining ground, the Algerian troops, led with remarkable élan, retook it. The Algerian Division's gaining of Monte Belvedere and Monte Abate is an example of a battle won by sheer strength of will as much as by weapons and tactical skill. One incident shows the spirit of the Division, and the strength of the relationship between its officers and men, that helped to win it this battle. Lieutenant Bouakkaz had sworn to be the first to reach the summit of Point 862, but early in the attack he was struck dead by a German bullet. This threatened to undermine the morale of his platoon, who faltered. Immediately two NCOs picked up his body and, sitting it on a rifle held between them and with a third soldier supporting its back, they carried it forward in the charge, galvanising the men who then followed them to the summit, and ensuring that their officer kept his oath.[18] For long periods, the Algerians fought without food and water, and with dwindling supplies of ammunition, their mule columns destroyed or pinned down by German fire. They held a decisive advantage in their own fire support, however: three regiments of Algerian artillery equipped with 105mm and 155mm howitzers, supported by a US Field Artillery Brigade of six battalions similarly equipped. On occasions when attacks threatened to overrun them, the forward observers called down artillery fire on their own positions, this being the only way to break up the German attacks and hold the ground when the Algerian infantry's ammunition was running out. By the end of January, the Germans could no longer afford to counter-attack, their battalions now reduced to little more than a hundred men. Juin's units had also suffered heavily, and Monte Abate and Monte Belvedere had cost the 4th Tunisian Infantry alone over 1,300 men, or more than half of its effective strength. On 29 January, Juin reported to Clark that his 2nd Moroccan and 3rd Algerian Divisions were both fully engaged, and that the Algerian Division, its reserves committed, could attack for a further twenty-four hours, but no more. He needed support urgently from the US II Corps to the south, to ensure that his Algerians on Belvedere were not isolated. The French Expeditionary Corps was spent.

The Americans Break into Cassino: the 34th Division
The US II Corps had as its objectives Monte Castellone (Point 771) and Colle San Angelo (Point 601) and the Albaneta Farm (Point 468). Over the three-mile distance from Monte Castellone to Monte Cassino, two ridges offered approaches to an attacker attempting to outflank Monte Cassino from the north. One ridge descended southwards from Monte Castellone for about 1,500 yards to Point 706 where it forked into two spurs. One spur led to the south-west through Colle St Angelo to Point 575, then turned south-east towards the monastery. The other spur descended south from Point 706 to a small valley where lay Albaneta Farm. Another ridge ran parallel to that between Monte Castellone and Point 706; this one, 'Snakeshead Ridge', began at Colle Majola (Point 481) and ran south and south-west to Point 593, then descended east towards Cassino town.

Most of the 25,000 inhabitants of Cassino had been evacuated. Until then, it had been a thriving market town extending for about three-quarters of a mile. Mid-way between Naples and Rome, which was some 85 miles to the north-west, Cassino was popular with visitors and prospered as a result. It was also an important railway centre on Italy's main north-south line, with its station to the south of the town on the other side of Highway 6. Behind the town was a hill, the Rocca Janicula, with the remains of a medieval castle. Allied soldiers would know this as 'Castle Hill' (Point 193). A saddle of rock linked it to Monte Cassino,

Monte Cassino, the monastery in ruins. Note the thickness of the walls that so concerned General Tuker of 4th Indian Division.

and this marked the start of the shortest, but most difficult, route to climb the larger height. On the south-eastern point of steep-sided Monte Cassino stood the great buildings of the famous Benedictine monastery, a huge four-storeyed structure in cream-coloured stone. Built like a fortress with a thick battlemented base and rows of small windows, it enclosed five cloistered courtyards and extended for some 220 yards on its longest side. From the town, a winding road ascended the eastern slope for six miles through seven hairpin bends to reach the monastery. Just short of the crest, this road passed a cone-shaped feature, Point 435. Here, later, a shell-smashed cable-car support would resemble a gallows; to Allied soldiers this would be 'Hangman's Hill'.

Yet, at the beginning of 1944, no scrutiny with the naked eye from a distance or through field glasses, nor reference to any map, could reveal the devilish nature of these sloping heights around Cassino. They were an attacker's nightmare, the rocky ground broken by unsuspected clefts and hollows with impenetrable patches of thorn and scrub, and littered with boulders. For an attacker, movement and observation in such terrain was near impossible, and the direction, momentum and cohesion of an attack could all quickly be lost. The lines of approach, the number of troops able to move along them, and the frontage of an attack; the ground dictated them all. To speak of attacks by divisions, brigades or battalions in such country means little, as in reality only a company or platoon, or less, could move forward at a time. For the defence, this was a great advantage, for it was possible to accentuate the natural obstacles of the ground with minefields and belts of barbed wire and, where feasible, the flooding of low ground. Thereby the attacking troops could be channelled into lines of approach under the defender's guns, previously registered by artillery and mortars, that became highly effective killing grounds.

Once Kesselring had identified the Cassino area as the lynchpin of the Gustav Line Hitler decreed that it should be of 'fortress' strength. Thereafter, the skill and ingenuity of several engineer and construction battalions, and the labour of some 44,000 Todt Organisation workers, turned the Cassino sector into one of the most formidable defensive systems of the entire war. There was extensive use of barbed wire, and a liberal use of mines. These included numerous shrapnel-burst anti-personnel mines, detonated by pressure or trip wires and capable of painfully removing a victim's foot or genitals. Many were 'box mines', as Allied troops termed them, and very difficult to detect as they had wooden casings and few metal parts.

North of Cassino the Germans dammed the River Rapido, flooding the valley for several miles, and heavily mined both banks. Throughout the Liri and Rapido Valleys villages, farmhouses and buildings became strongpoints incorporated into the defensive zone. Many had their ground floors turned into bunker positions with layers of logs and crushed stone capable of protecting their occupants from direct artillery hits. Tank turrets were dug-in, and camouflaged. Good fields of fire were created by clearing trees, their stumps left as tank obstacles, and anti-tank ditches were dug. In November 1943, the OKW had allocated 100 steel shelters, with which to line large dugouts, and some 76 portable armoured pillboxes. These were dome-shaped and six feet in height, but dug-in to leave three feet above ground, and could accommodate two men with a heavy machine-gun.

In Cassino town itself there was a lavish use of concrete and steel as buildings became strongpoints, their cellars and ground floors reinforced to withstand heavy bombardment. There were many tunnels and connecting trenches dug between them, often linking buildings on opposite sides of a road, with positions designed and sited for mutual support with interlocking fields of fire. Well-camouflaged tanks lay hidden within some of the larger buildings, and some buildings also had concealed bunkers and pillboxes built inside them. The town became an attacker's death trap, a fortified maze that could only succumb to prolonged and costly street fighting.

Monte Cassino and the surrounding mountain positions provided the Germans with excellent observation of Allied movement, from which to direct the fire of their supporting artillery and mortars located farther to the rear. These heights also became part of the fortified zone. Engineers and construction teams used explosives to blast gun emplacements and machine-gun and mortar positions out of the rock, also sited for mutual support, which were then protected with the ubiquitous concrete and steel. Where gullies and ravines offered some protection from their fields of fire, the Germans mined and wired them extensively. Caves, dynamited out of the hillside and strengthened, protected their crews from air and artillery bombardment, and from the worst of the winter weather. Skilful camouflage covered all on the hillsides, and many of these German positions would reveal themselves to Allied troops only by their lethality.

For his attack on this fortress, Keyes had as his II Corps striking force nine infantry battalions of the 133rd, 135th and 168th Regiments of General Ryder's 34th Division. There were also three tank battalions, though the terrain was hardly suited to their use. Of critical importance was the II Corps firepower, in this case seventeen battalions of artillery, including two equipped with heavy 240mm howitzers capable of effective plunging fire in the mountains.

Late on 24 January, the 133rd began the first stage of the attack, to cross the Rapido two miles north of Cassino and seize Monte Villa, where lay the shell-battered ruins of buildings thought to be a former barracks, and the low hills Points 56 and 213. Two miles farther to the north lay Cairo village. Intending to cross the Rapido with two battalions supported by the 54 Sherman medium tanks of the 756th Tank Battalion, the 133rd's attack soon stalled amid exploding mines and the sodden ground in which the tanks became bogged. Heavy fire came down from Monte Villa, held by the battalions of the German 132nd Grenadier Regiment. Next morning, under cover of heavy artillery support, the 133rd's battalions got several platoons across the river. By midnight on 25 January they had a small bridgehead, but under heavy fire throughout the next day the troops could only take cover and could not advance beyond the river. Early on 27 January the 135th attempted to cross on the 133rd's left, but boggy ground frustrated the tanks, and the single infantry company that crossed the river struggled in vain, in the darkness and under fire, against flooded ground, mines, and wire obstacles. Once across the river, the American troops simply could not close with their enemy, and until they could do so, the attack was bound to fail.

Keyes was now urging Ryder to get troops beyond the river into the mountains, and the next move that morning was an attempt to pass the 168th Infantry through the 133rd's bridgehead from where they would strike out at Point 213. Preceded by an hour's artillery bombardment, two battalions were to attack abreast, each preceded by a platoon of tanks to break the wire, explode anti-personnel mines and engage strongpoints. The approaches for the tanks were narrow, with stretches under water, and several slipped off. Eventually four Shermans got across, having churned the ground so much that others were unable to follow until engineers repaired the route. By afternoon all four were knocked out, three by fire and one by a mine, but by dark the 168th had five companies across. One of these ascended Point 213, but its commander, believing the position would become untenable in daylight, began to move his men back. What happened next amounted to a tragedy; control broke down and confusion and uncertainty set in, causing troops enduring the stress of a difficult battle to panic. The withdrawal degenerated into chaos as men fled back across the river. Confusion and panic spreads as fast as a forest fire, and is just as hard to stop; other companies witnessing the flight soon joined in, and only on the near bank was order eventually restored. Only two companies were left on the far bank, exposed to fire, and these were deliberately withdrawn, but re-crossed the river farther north and probed towards Cairo village.

Tanks were the solution; if they could only negotiate the ground they would assist the infantry over the river and across the mile and a half of level river plain to the hills. All efforts were made to that end, Keyes assigning all his engineers to the 34th Division and Ryder, in turn, directing them to ensure serviceable tank routes for his next attempt. On 29 January, again under cover of a heavy artillery bombardment, and led by Shermans of the 760th Tank Battalion, the three battalions of the 168th Infantry crossed the river. Seven tanks got across, two of which were soon knocked out by German fire, but the others enabled the infantry to make progress. In the afternoon, a further 23 Shermans of the 756th Tank Battalion crossed successfully. Firing more than 1,000 rounds of 75mm high explosive at near point-blank range into German positions and smashing wire obstacles, their guns shot the infantry forward on to the slopes. Early on 30 January, Points 213 and 56 were captured, and subsequently held against the inevitable German counter-attacks, and Cairo village was also taken. The tanks, unable to move on to the slopes of the higher ground, were now helpless, remaining at the base of the hills to avoid the German anti-tank and artillery fire that sought them.

For both sides the Cassino sector was now, at the beginning of February 1944, the focal point of the Gustav Line battle, and both Kesselring and Alexander faced the problem of finding more troops for it. It was above all a question of infantry. At the end of January, von Senger began to concentrate available units of the 90th Panzer Grenadier Division in the Cassino area, initially three battalions, and placed the Divisional Commander, the dynamic Major-General Ernst Günther Baade, in overall command. The 4th Alpine Battalion, an independent unit, was also deployed to the sector. On 3 February Kesselring decided to transfer the 1st Parachute Division from LXXVI Panzer Corps, and its units began to arrive in Cassino, the 3rd/3rd Parachute Regiment, 2nd/1st Parachute Regiment and the Parachute Machine Gun Battalion. The paratroops were élite troops, knew it, and were determined to prove it to their comrades and enemies alike. Their presence in the strong Cassino defences would prove one of military history's most formidable combinations.

Alexander's problem was as acute as Kesselring's. Clark's main Fifth Army was weakened by infantry casualties, and by the need to reinforce the Anzio beachhead to which the British 56th Division was sent from X Corps, and the US 45th Division from Clark's reserve. There was nothing left with which to reinforce the 34th Division at Cassino and provide the essential exploitation force for the Liri Valley. Alexander decided, like Kesselring, to take what he needed from the Adriatic sector. On the same day that Kesselring made his decision to send the Paratroop Division to Cassino, 3 February, Alexander formed the New Zealand Corps, comprising Major-General Howard Kippenberger's 2nd New Zealand Division and Major-General Francis Tuker's 4th Indian Division. He also earmarked the British 78th Division for the New Zealand Corps and exploitation in the Liri Valley. All these formations were from Leese's Eighth Army, where their loss was sorely felt. As Leese reported to Alexander, not only was he prevented from mounting any offensive in his sector, but the removal of these units undermined his ability to relieve formations desperately in need of rest and reorganisation. For Alexander, however, it was 'urgently necessary' to force the Germans out of their Cassino position and open the Liri Valley to enable a link-up between Fifth Army and the force at Anzio; this remained the overriding imperative.[19] Placed under the command of General Bernard Freyberg, the New Zealand Corps began to take over part of II Corps' front south of Cassino on 6 February. Like the German paratroops they would soon confront, the 2nd New Zealand and 4th Indian Divisions were, as far as the British Army acknowledges such, élite formations, highly experienced and with impressive fighting records.

In the meantime, the US 34th Division was fighting its heart out in the high ground around Cassino and in the town itself. Renewing the attack on 1 February, under cover of heavy fog, the 3rd/135th secured Point 771 on Monte Castellone and the 2nd/135th captured Colle Majola. By 3 February, these battalions

> **XIV PANZER CORPS DEFENCE OF CASSINO AREA, 6–12 FEBRUARY 1944[20]**
>
> **Units of 71st Infantry, 90th Panzer Grenadier, 44th Infantry, and 1st Parachute Divisions**
>
> *Area north of Cassino* opposing US 34th Division: 131st, 132nd, 134th Grenadier Regiments of 44th Infantry Division, seriously depleted. Elements of 90th Panzer Grenadier Division, (i.e. 2nd/200th PGR) and 1st Parachute Division taking over.
>
> Some specific locations:
> *Cassino Town:* 211th Grenadier Regiment (71st Infantry Division)
> *Monte Castellone (Point 771) area:* 4th Alpine Battalion,
> *Colle Majola (Point 481) – Points 593/569 area:* 3rd/3rd Parachute Regiment; 2nd/1st Parachute Regiment; Para MG Bn; 1st/361st PGR (90th PG Div)
> *Colle San Angelo (Point 601) area:* 3rd/361st PGR

had troops on Points 445 and 706, but fierce German counter-attacks prevented further advance. Late on 5 February the battalions of the 168th Infantry were committed to an attack from Point 445 south towards Monte Cassino, but were stopped by fire from interlocking German positions. By now, von Senger had committed the 4th Alpine Battalion, the 3rd Parachute Battalion and a battalion of panzer grenadiers to hold these heights. As the American troops fought their way closer towards Highway 6 and the Liri Valley, the imperative for the Germans to halt them became more desperate. The fighting became intense, small-unit thrust and counter-thrust on the slopes and ridges. Unable to dig-in on the rocky ground, the American troops protected themselves with piled stones. They were frequently pinned by German fire to these positions, where they endured for prolonged periods the cold and the wet, with intermittent supplies of food, water and ammunition. German positions were often only a few yards away, and casualties on both sides were heavy. The American battalions now had all the men they could gather from the non-combatant elements of the division in their rifle companies, while the Germans reported grievous losses to the superior American artillery that fired unceasingly.

Street Fighting: Cassino Town

The battalions of the 133rd Infantry secured Monte Villa and moved south towards Cassino, and in the afternoon of 3 February the 1st and 3rd Battalions, supported by tanks, broke into the northern outskirts of the town. A fierce and prolonged battle followed, in and around the town. Castle Hill (Point 193) was captured but lost to a counter-attack, though the north-west slopes and nearby Point 165 were held. In Cassino itself, tank support and the use of smoke enabled the troops of the 3rd Battalion to gain their initial foothold. Under cover of tank fire the infantry filled in anti-tank ditches and removed mines to help the tanks forward, but every building they encountered was fortified. With their bazookas well forward to repel German tanks, few of which were encountered, the US troops blasted their way into the buildings, but were soon fighting, floor by floor and room by room. Unable to approach doors or windows, well covered by fire, bazookas were used to blast entrances through the thick walls; then a small party, covered by others, would approach and throw in grenades. A battalion of

the 133rd Infantry later recorded that it used an average of 500 grenades a day in this fighting at Cassino. A typical method of house clearing employed by its troops was to throw a grenade into a room and then immediately after it had exploded to burst into the room firing automatic weapons. Any Germans left alive were found lying on the floor with no fight left.[21] Tank fire or artillery levelled buildings so well fortified as to deny approach, but the ensuing rubble provided excellent cover for the defenders. It was slow, nerve-wracking and costly fighting, and the defence was such that gains could be measured only in yards.

From 8 to 12 February the 34th Division, with the 142nd and 141st Regiments of the 36th Division, reinforced since the Rapido crossing attempt, made their final effort to break the Cassino stronghold. The battalions of the 135th and 168th Regiments, and the 141st of 36th Division, fought to reach Monte Cassino and secure Points 569 and 593, a savage battle of attack and counter-attack fought in rain and sleet against the four German battalions fighting equally hard to retain these heights. Point 593 changed hands three times in as many days, and the Americans reached within 1,000 yards of the monastery itself. Troops of the 36th Division attacked towards and reached the Albaneta Farm. Here too the fighting was furious and desperate, the attacking US troops using 1,500 grenades in a single day, and although the German defence nearly broke, it was reinforced in time and the attack was held. The northern edge of the Liri Valley, just a mile and a half away, remained out of reach.

In Cassino town the 133rd Infantry, despite its efforts and fire support, was unable to gain more than its tenuous hold on the northern edge. While this battle was raging in early February, Alexander sent his deputy, the American General Lemnitzer, to II Corps to report on its situation. Alexander was concerned at the punishment the Corps was taking, and Lemnitzer confirmed that its troops were exhausted and must soon be given a respite. In fact morale was suffering under the combination of hard fighting, extreme fatigue, heavy casualties, and cruel weather. Perhaps worse was the disheartening sense of frustration among soldiers who knew they had given all and more than could be expected of them. As soldiers, they assessed their enemy as formidable, but knew themselves to be a match for him, yet they now knew that however close they came to their objectives, there just was not the strength left in their

Left: British troops move through the ruins of Cassino town. Note the mix of standard infantry weapons. The soldier in the foreground carries his Lee-Enfield No. 1 Mk III rifle, the soldier walking at the end of the file and the soldier crouching in the background both appear to have the later No. 4 Mk. I version. The soldier in the centre carries his Thompson sub-machine gun, a weapon extensively used by the British Army. The photograph also indicates the formidable defensive potential of the buildings and rubble in the town.

> **STATE OF US 34TH AND 36TH INFANTRY DIVISIONS, 12 FEBRUARY 1944**[22]
>
> **36th Division:** Infantry regiments each reduced to less than 25% effective strength.
>
> **34th Division:**
> 3rd/133rd   reduced to 140 in three rifle companies
> 100th/133rd   reduced to 85 in three rifle companies
> 168th Infantry   reduced to 793 in three battalions
> 135th Infantry   reduced to average of 30 in each rifle company.

units to secure them. Yet neither Clark nor Keyes was keen to hand over the battle to Freyberg's Corps if there was the least chance of the American troops succeeding. Alexander, against his better judgement and presumably for reasons of coalition politics, did not insist. Following Lemnitzer's report, however, he decided that II Corps could not prolong its attack after 12 February, and must be relieved by Freyberg's New Zealand Corps. The American soldiers of II Corps had, by German admission, come very close to success, 'within a bare 100 metres' in von Senger's own words and, also by German admission they had inflicted crippling losses on the German battalions committed against them. On 9 February von Senger reckoned that his casualties were some 300 men per day.[23] The end of the first battle of Cassino had come not a day too soon for either side, and for the Allies that was the pity of it.

It is a very hard thing to have to concede the field. The battle-hardened troops of the New Zealand and Indian Divisions were sobered and appalled when they saw the conditions under which the Americans had fought, and the state of the men they relieved. Many, weakened by exhaustion and exposure to the cold and wet, remained at their posts and had to be assisted out of their positions and carried down the hillsides on stretchers. Some never left their posts at all. In 1948, a party of British officers on an army battlefield tour of the heights around Cassino came across the skeleton of a man crouched against some rocks in the way that an infantryman would take guard with his weapon. Beside it lay rusting an American helmet and rifle.[24]

5

THE SECOND AND THIRD BATTLES OF CASSINO

The experience of the first battle clearly indicated that attacking in Italy required a local superiority of at least three-to-one in infantry in order to have a reasonable chance of successfully penetrating well-constructed and organised defences. In fact, as was acknowledged at the time, infantry strength proved the most reliable indicator of offensive or defensive capability.[1] Tanks, while they could prove extremely valuable for fire support, had few such opportunities. Where they could not manoeuvre or were without infantry in support, they were as likely to be liabilities. In the first battle, Clark's Fifth Army had been strong enough to break into the Gustav Line, but not through it. In focusing upon the entrance to the Liri Valley at Cassino, the plan also had a rigidity, due mainly to the time imperative, preventing the exploitation of success either to the north or the south of the Cassino position. Both McCreery's X Corps on the Garigliano, and Juin's French Corps to the north were intended to fix German strength to enable II Corps to break quickly into the Liri Valley. Only after the failure of the 36th Division at the Rapido did the emphasis change to one of outflanking the Cassino position from the north. By then, Juin and Keyes had sufficient troops only to fight their way to within sight of the Liri Valley before casualties and exhaustion forced a halt. With the relief of II Corps by Freyberg's New Zealand Corps, Alexander and Clark were about to commit fresh divisions, but only two of them, against the formidable defensive zone at Cassino that – to paraphrase Kesselring – had already broken the teeth of two divisions.

Time remained the principal reason, as Alexander made clear in his Operation Instruction of 11 February. Exploitation into the Liri Valley required a spell of dry weather to harden the ground for armour, and suitable weather for air support. Yet, it was necessary to secure a bridgehead over the Rapido near Cassino and to clear the Germans from the nearby heights before any such exploitation could take place.[2] So the battle at Cassino would continue. Hindsight is the harshest of critics. Especially when fuelled by indignation at the apparent callousness and stupidity of commanders prolonging the agony of troops sent into a hopeless battle. Alexander and Clark, however, hardly had the perception of the battle they were fighting that survivors and historians would convey to later generations. What was their picture in early 1944? There must have been a feeling that success was at hand. However scornful later critics would be, this was an important factor at the time. Since late January Enigma decrypts were indicating the desperate situation of the XIV Panzer Corps as it fought to withstand the attack of II Corps north and west of Cassino town. The last local reserves were in the German line, and a signal of 4 February revealed that Headquarters troops were fighting in the front line as well.[3] This was an

> **General Bernard Freyberg (later 1st Baron Freyberg).** A holder of the Victoria Cross earned for exceptional leadership and bravery fighting against the German offensive on the Western Front in 1918, Freyberg became one of the most experienced field commanders in British and Commonwealth forces during the Second World War. He commanded the New Zealand Division during the abortive campaign in Greece and Churchill appointed him commander of the British and Commonwealth garrison on the island of Crete, where he conducted a spirited defence against the ultimately successful German airborne invasion in 1941. He commanded the New Zealand Division in North Africa and later X Corps. He was directly responsible to the New Zealand Government for the employment of his division that contained a sizeable proportion of the country's male population eligible for military service. Freyberg, like his Division, was prepared to face any task, however difficult, but he was equally determined not to waste the lives of his men.

army in crisis that could stand little more pressure and was about to break, and Clark's signal to Alexander on 2 February that 'Present indications are that the Cassino heights will be captured very soon' was not without foundation. The problem was that II Corps had fought itself out bringing the Germans to the far edge of crisis, and lacked the strength to topple them into disaster. It was reasonable to suppose that two battle-hardened but fresh divisions, one of them trained for mountain warfare (4th Indian), might do it.

If, as it appeared, Cassino and the immediate heights were within grasp, then this would be the quickest way of unlocking Highway 6 and the Liri Valley. The battering of II Corps that concerned Alexander indicated how hard and costly the fighting would be. In February 1944, however, with the Bernhardt Line battles and the initial attempts at the Gustav Line behind them, Allied commanders well knew the consequences of attacking in Italy. The Bernhardt Line battles indicated that eventually the Germans, suffering equally under the pressure of incessant fighting, would eventually crack under the strain – and at Cassino there was evidence that they were on the verge of doing so. To grant the Germans a reprieve when the Americans had fought their way to within yards of Monte Cassino and a mile and a half from Highway 6, would be to waste all the effort and lives that had been expended. However hard the battle, there were fresh troops to hand for it, and they would now be fighting with a hard-won breakthrough in sight, or so it must have seemed in February 1944. If there is a parallel here with the attitude of senior commanders on the Western Front during the First World War, it is because in Italy Alexander and Clark, and even Kesselring and von Senger, faced similar problems. In fact, compressed in space and time, Alexander's problem was probably the more acute in February 1944. While the arithmetic of attrition was harsh, the alternative would be to accept a German-imposed stalemate, of no help to 'Overlord'. Nor was this an option with the Allied beachhead at Anzio under imminent threat. As well as indicating the critical condition of XIV Panzer Corps at Cassino, Enigma decrypts were keeping Alexander and Clark well informed of Kesselring's plans

One of the British Commonwealth's most distinguished soldiers: Lieutenant-General Sir Bernard Freyberg VC who commanded the New Zealand Corps during the second and third battles of Cassino. Freyberg's field car, upon which he is standing, is one of the ubiquitous Jeeps that served in a variety of roles with allied forces in every theatre of the Second World War. Note the New Zealand pennant visible just above the bonnet. The vehicle in the left background appears to be a Bedford ambulance.

for von Mackensen to launch a major attack upon the beachhead.[4] It would have been unthinkable to remove the pressure on the Gustav Line at the point which offered a rapid move along Highway 6 to the Liri Valley, when there was a good chance that that point was about to fall. To maintain the attack at Cassino, would not only be likely to bring a breakthrough, but also relieve the pressure on the Anzio beachhead by preventing von Vietinghoff and von Senger from releasing forces for it.

Freyberg's First Attempt: Operation 'Avenger'
Taking over the Cassino sector from II Corps confronted Freyberg with an unenviable prospect. First, the 4th Indian Division had to take over the forward American positions on the heights, a difficult and time-consuming process over poor roads and trails many of which were registered by German artillery and mortars. Given the confusion of the fighting on the slopes during the latter stages of the II Corps attack, it was by no means clear precisely who held what feature. On 12 February, the Germans launched a counter-attack devised by Baade and sanctioned by von Senger. It was a desperate move intended to gain a respite from the American pressure, and the American artillery supported by the guns of New Zealand Corps shattered it. However, in the close fighting on the heights German troops did regain much of Point 593, a fact unknown to the Indian Division.

Freyberg's problem was how to unlock the Cassino position. It would prove the toughest proposition of his distinguished military career. Initially considered was the deployment of 4th Indian Division in a wide flanking movement to the north of Cassino and Monte Castellone, supported farther to the north by Juin, combined with a New Zealand brigade attack from Colle Majola towards the Albaneta Farm, while more New Zealand infantry and armour stood by to break into the Liri Valley. This concept reflected the views of the mountain-experienced Tuker, and would have exploited the strengths of his division, but by 9 February it was discarded in favour of a straightforward continuation of the American attacks. This was not simply a case of a sound plan sacrificed on the altar of time. By 9 February, although Alexander was justifiably concerned about the state of II Corps, its attacks appeared to be on the very edge of success. It therefore made sense to use the Indians and New Zealanders to make the final effort of which the by now fought-out Americans were incapable, from the ground that the Americans had won. There were two other factors working against the original idea of a wide flanking move through the mountains. One was that its most influential advocate, Tuker, was incapacitated by illness and confined to his headquarters caravan. Brigadier Dimoline assumed command of 4th Indian Division, though Tuker remained at hand to give guidance and advice. The other was that, despite its advantage of turning the German Cassino position, the plan carried great risk. It required the achievement of surprise to gain momentum through terrain all-too-easily blocked by the Germans, and it depended upon mule supply columns sustaining the troops over several miles of very difficult ground. While the 1,500 mules available to New Zealand Corps might be sufficient to do this for a brigade, they were certainly not enough for a division. There was also the risk of counter-attack, especially from German units concentrated in the Liri Valley, holding the advance in the mountains. Juin

> **4TH INDIAN DIVISION FEBRUARY 1944[5]**
>
> *7th Infantry Brigade*   1st Royal Sussex, 4th/16th Punjab, 1st/2nd Gurkha Rifles
> *5th Infantry Brigade*   1st/4th Essex, 4th/6th Rajputana Rifles, 1st/9th Gurkha Rifles.
> *11th Infantry Brigade*   2nd Cameron Highlanders, 1st/6th Rajputana Rifles, 2nd/7th Gurkha Rifles
>
> *Fire Support troops:* three field regiments of artillery, an anti-tank regiment and a light anti-aircraft regiment. Medium machine-guns of the MG Battalion, 6th Rajputana Rifles. Tanks of the Central India Horse.

and his staff, confronting these uncertainties with their North African mountain troops, might not have hesitated, but theirs was a mountain warfare expertise not possessed by New Zealand Corps.

In the plan finally adopted, following the relief of the US 34th Division by 4th Indian Division, the 7th Indian Brigade was to attack from Point 593 to secure Point 569 and 444 and reach the monastery. With this ground secured and taken over by 5th Indian Brigade, the 7th was to advance down towards Highway 6 and then turn east to attack Cassino town, already under attack from the south-east by the New Zealand Division. This effort was initially intended to start on the night 13/14 February.

The Monastery

So far, the monastery on Monte Cassino had remained largely unscathed by the fighting that raged in the valley and on the slopes below. Such odd artillery rounds and mortar bombs that had fallen in or near its precincts had been unintentional. To the Allied soldiers in the valley below, over which it seemed to brood menacingly, the monastery began to exercise perhaps an inevitable, but powerful, hold upon their imaginations. Indeed, there can have been few battlefields in the history of war so dominated by a building of religious significance, and its influence extended beyond its obvious physical presence deep into men's consciousness. In his graphic account of Cassino published in 1945, Fred Majdalany wrote that 'Those who fought at Cassino will remember above all the monastery founded by St Benedict. They will remember as long as they live how it dominated and overshadowed their bodies and their minds during the winter of 1944.'[6] In fact, for many it had become an object of hatred, accentuated by the belief that it was a venerable shrine of Christianity deliberately misused. Many were convinced at the time, and remained convinced long after the war, that the Germans were exploiting the immunity accorded the monastery by using its buildings as observation posts from which to direct their artillery fire. 'It was evil somehow,' remembered Sergeant Evans of 2nd London Irish, a battalion of the 78th Division. 'I don't know how a monastery can be evil, but it was looking at you. It was all-devouring if you like – a sun-bleached colour, grim. It had a terrible hold on us soldiers. I don't think I was convinced that the Germans were *firing* from there, but it was such a wonderful observation post.'[7]

Although Monte Cassino was a heavily defended feature within the Gustav Line, German commanders including von Senger and Kesselring consistently and vigorously denied that troops had been stationed inside the monastery itself. In fact, they posted military police to prevent unauthorised entry. The abbot of the time, Abbot Diamare, confirmed these assertions and despite considerable investigation, the Allies subsequently could discover no evidence worth the name with which to refute them. They have long since been accepted as the truth. In fact, military logic argued against having troops and equipment positioned for defence in the monastery when it was intact. Freyberg himself later acknowledged that such troops would have been vulnerable and that 'Nobody wants to sit on an obvious target.'[8] As an observation post, von Senger later recalled that apart from a repugnance to misuse the monastery in such a way, it would have made no sense. It was far too conspicuous, and likely to be neutralised by heavy fire during battle.[9] The observation posts that caused such grief to Allied troops were no doubt those skilfully camouflaged on the mountain slopes.

The crucial issue in early February 1944 was neither whether the Germans were occupying the monastery, nor the conviction among Allied soldiers that they were. It was how to clear the Monte Cassino position as a whole, and how the Germans might use the monastery buildings if 4th Indian Division's attack looked likely to succeed. Tuker was deeply unhappy that his division should make a direct attack upon such a formidable defensive zone, known to contain heavily fortified emplacements and that had already repulsed the Americans with heavy casualties. As late as 12 February he still advocated an outflanking move. In the first of two letters sent to New Zealand Corps Headquarters that day, he observed that by using Monte Castellone and the area held by the US II Corps as a firm base, it would be possible to attack in 'fast short jabs' to the west and south-west of Monte Castellone and cut Highway 6 west of Monte Cassino. This, combined with an attack on Cassino town to contain its garrison and linked up with a crossing of the river below Cassino, would isolate the Monte Cassino position.

Tuker made his views quite clear in this letter. If, he argued instead of such an outflanking move, a direct assault was to be attempted, Monte Cassino would require softening up by 'a thorough and prolonged air bombardment' using 'really heavy bombs a good deal larger than "Kittybomber" missiles.'[10] Tuker was arguing for the bombardment of the entire position, but in his second letter he emphasised the importance of the monastery. Much to his frustration, his division received no intelligence about the buildings, but one of his staff had discovered an old book about the monastery in a Naples bookshop, revealing its fortress-like construction. Whether the monastery was then occupied by the Germans or not, Tuker argued, it was certain that it would be held as a defensive position against his division's attack, and to prevent this it would have to be demolished. Tuker demanded of his corps commander with justification, if somewhat peremptorily, information at once about how this fortress was to be dealt with, as his division lacked the capacity to do it. He argued that to ensure its destruction, 'block-buster' bombs should be applied against it.[11] In his reference to this weapon, Tuker clearly envisaged such a weight of bombing that little should be left of the buildings that would be of any use as a defensive position.[12]

Tuker's views and his urgency were those of a divisional commander the lives of whose men were about to be placed at great risk, in an attack in which he had little faith. His concerns were legitimate, but the decision to employ heavy bombers of the strategic air forces against Monte Cassino was neither for him nor for Freyberg to make. The Allies acknowledged the historical and cultural significance of many buildings and monuments in Italy. They did not intend to see them wantonly destroyed, and before leaving the theatre Eisenhower had provided firm guidance to Allied army commanders. In a message dated 29 December 1943, he stated that 'If we have to choose between destroying a famous building and sacrificing our own men, then our men's lives count infinitely more and the buildings must go.' He added, however, that 'military necessity' must not be allowed to cloak military or personal convenience.[13] The monastery on Monte Cassino presented Allied commanders with a stark and difficult choice about military necessity. On one hand to accept the risks identified by Tuker and perhaps later face the charge that they had failed to do all in their power to safeguard the lives of their men. On the other to bear the responsibility for destroying one of Europe's greatest cultural treasures. Freyberg firmly supported Tuker, warning that any higher commander who refused to authorise the request would have to be prepared to accept the responsibility for the failure of the attack.[14]

This was aimed primarily at his Army Commander, Clark, who did not want the monastery bombed. Clark was satisfied that the Germans were not occupying its buildings, and he was convinced that to bomb the monastery would be politically and militarily counter-productive, but he reluctantly acquiesced in view of his Corps commander's resolve. Had his Corps commander been a fellow American, however, he would not have sanctioned the bombing. Clark as a commander of a coalition army was now up against men who, although his subordinates, held considerable stature as highly experienced and distinguished soldiers within the British Army. An army, moreover, in which it was acceptable for officers of their rank to question and discuss their operations in such a way. It would have been inconceivable for American officers such as Lucas, bound for Anzio, or Walker facing his task at the Rapido, to have acted with Tuker's forcefulness, however unhappy about their orders, and however justified. Freyberg's stature and influence also had a political dimension and implication; he was directly responsible to an Allied government for how his troops were employed, that of New Zealand. It was a very delicate issue.

Clark's own superior and Army Group Commander, Alexander, faced the decision with firm equanimity. The lives of Allied soldiers came first, and he supported Freyberg. The necessary diversion of the heavy bombers away from their strategic targets in order to attack the monastery would normally have required the sanction of the Allied Supreme Commander in the Mediterranean, General Sir Henry Maitland Wilson. Presumably, he gave it, though there is no record of his participation in the decision.[15] The request passed to the Allied air forces. General Ira Eaker commanding the Mediterranean Allied Air Forces, and his deputy, Air Chief Marshal Sir John Slessor, did not relish the job, but prepared to assist the soldiers through the Gustav Line to the Liri Valley. On 14 February, two senior American officers, Eaker himself and Lieutenant General Jacob Devers, Wilson's deputy commander, flew low over the monastery in a Piper Cub observation plane. This was safe enough, given that the Germans rarely fired on such planes spotting for the Allied artillery, for fear of revealing their gun positions. Eaker and Devers wanted to see for themselves whether the Germans were using the monastery. Flying over the buildings for about ten minutes, they saw what they believed to be a German military aerial in the inner courtyard, and German soldiers moving in and out of the buildings. They also noted the German positions that were very close to the monastery, and this is really the point. The Germans, who had incorporated Monte Cassino, but not the monastery buildings surmounting it, into their Gustav Line, presented the moral dilemma to the Allies and for this it is unreasonable to blame them. It is inconceivable that the Germans would not have used Monte Cassino in this way, if they were to deny the Liri Valley and Highway 6 to the Allies. They could no more have been expected to deny themselves Monte Cassino for the sake of the monastery than the Allies could have been expected to place their soldiers at risk for its sake. However scrupulous the Germans were about not using the monastery, it stood upon ground used for defence. That ground could not be neutralised by firepower, and certainly not by heavy bombing, without imperilling the buildings even if not deliberately targeted. Furthermore, there was sufficient doubt within the Allied command about whether the Germans were using the buildings, and the use they might make of them as the fighting progressed, and there was the important factor of morale. Senior Allied commanders could hardly have justified sending their men against Monte Cassino without bombing the monastery, knowing its psychological hold on their troops. The question had already been raised by war correspondents in the British and US press, whose reports, reflecting the views of the troops, were hostile to the monastery, and the immunity thus far accorded it. It is hard to see how the request from the attacking division, once made, could have been refused. It was a tragedy of war, but once the focus of Allied effort to open the Liri Valley became a direct attack upon Monte Cassino, rather than an outflanking move, the monastery was doomed.

A tragedy once decided upon, it was equally tragic that the bombing did nothing to assist the New Zealand Corps' attack. Clark was proved right in his conviction that the bombing would ultimately work to the German advantage, and not only in propaganda terms of presenting the Allies as barbaric. For such bombing to be of use to attacking troops, they had to be well placed to exploit it, and those of 4th Indian Division were not. The relief of the American troops of the 34th and 36th Divisions took longer than expected. It was soon discovered by 7th Indian Brigade that, instead of their attack starting from Point 593, they would first have to capture it, Baade's counter-attack having forced the Americans to a precarious hold on its northern slopes. Both Dimoline and Brigadier Lovett, commanding 7th Indian Brigade, realised that German troops on Point 593 could enfilade the right flank of any attack upon Monte Cassino; in their view it had to come first. The main attack on Monte Cassino was postponed to the night of 16/17 February, with 7th Brigade to make its preliminary attack on Point 593 on the night of 15th/16th. Then factors beyond the control of New Zealand Corps intervened. One was the weather forecast. Eaker and his air commanders were about to unleash heavy bombing against a pinpoint target in

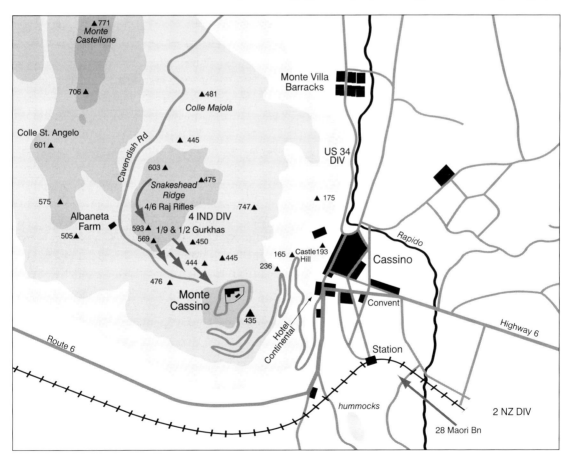

THE SECOND BATTLE OF MONTE CASSINO, 17/18 FEBRUARY 1944: 4th Indian Division on Monte Cassino and 2nd NZ Division at Cassino railway station ('Avenger')

close proximity to friendly troops. Their crews needed clear weather to ensure the maximum possible accuracy and 15 February would provide it, subsequent days would not. Moreover, after that date there could be no guarantee of providing bomber support at Cassino, and not only because of the weather. They would be on call to support the Anzio beachhead, against which Kesselring, as senior Allied commanders knew through Enigma decrypts, was about to launch his major attack. It had to be 15 February, but it was quite impossible for 4th Indian Division to bring forward its own timetable.

At about 0930 on 15 February the first of 135 B-17 Flying Fortresses arrived over Cassino and began to release their bombs on the monastery from 15,000–18,000 feet. They dropped 287 tons of 500lb general-purpose bombs, and 66 tons of 100lb incendiaries. They were followed by 47 B-25 Mitchell and 40 B-26 Marauder medium bombers which dropped a further 140 tons of 1,000lb bombs. The artillery of Fifth Army joined in.[16] Allied soldiers and war correspondents cheered as they watched the bombs fall, but not all of them. Juin, watching with a group of his senior French officers was heard to remark, 'No, they'll never get anywhere that way. The infantry will never be able to get forward amongst all that.'[17] Clark refused to watch. The forward troops of 7th Indian Brigade on the slopes below the monastery had little cause to cheer either. News of the bombing timetable had reached them through Fifth Army channels only minutes before the bombers arrived, giving them no time to pull back, and they had several casualties from falling masonry. A further tragedy was that the monks and several hundred Italian civilians that had sought safety from the fighting were inside the buildings when they were bombed. Fifth Army's guns had fired leaflets warning that the monastery would be taken under fire, though not stating when, and an evacuation was prepared for the 16 February. The bombing had come too early for them too, and some 300 died. German positions on Monte Cassino were shaken, but few if any casualties were inflicted upon their troops. The monastery was in ruins, but its outer walls, in some places thirty feet thick, and the main gateway remained. Tuker had been right about the scale of bombing and the type of bombs needed to prevent the monastery becoming a formidable defensive position. In the afternoon, as the Abbot led his survivors out, Baade's troops set up the first of their machine-gun positions in the ruins, and Tuker's fortress became a fact.

That night, the 1st Royal Sussex of 7th Indian Brigade attempted to seize Point 593. Their positions were some 500 yards from the crest, but only some 70 yards from German positions whose guns kept them pinned in daylight, unable to reconnoitre the ground. Only two platoons, some 70 men, of 'C' Company could deploy on the ridge to attack, and soon after dark they crept forward. There was no preliminary bombardment or support from mortars and machine-guns due to the nearness of the German positions, though artillery fired at alternative targets as a diversion. Somehow, after moving about 50 yards, German troops, no doubt alert and expecting trouble after the day's bombing, spotted them, and they came under heavy machine-gun fire and grenades. While small parties tried to crawl forward and around the German positions they could make no progress and soon exhausted their own stock of grenades, the only weapon they could use without giving away their positions in the dark. To avoid exposure in daylight, and certain death, they fell back, having taken 34 casualties.

Early next day, the 16th, Kesselring and von Mackensen launched Operation 'Fischfang' (Fish Catch), their major attack intended to destroy the Anzio beachhead, employing some 45 infantry battalions with heavy armour and artillery support. The imperative was now firmly on Fifth Army to relieve the pressure upon the beachhead by attacking the Gustav Line.

On the following night, 16/17 February, the 1st Royal Sussex tried again at Point 593, this time attempting to feed more troops into the attack. Extra grenades were to hand, but not as many as intended, and artillery engaged nearby peaks to prevent flanking fire. This was a difficult challenge for the gunners who had to skim their shells over the top of the Sussex, and some fell short among them. Despite this, the attack made better progress, overrunning some of the initial German positions and, despite heavy German fire, the difficult ground and the inevitable confusion, small parties of the Sussex reached the summit of Point 593. Then, during the fighting, a German soldier fired three green Very lights as a signal, possibly for reinforcements, but it also happened to be the Sussex's own signal for a withdrawal and the companies fell back, this time having taken 70 casualties.

Two days after the bombing of the monastery, the New Zealand Corps offensive had amounted to only two unsuccessful attacks upon a single feature by little more than a company of a single battalion. With the Anzio beachhead force now fighting for its survival, and with Clark and Alexander increasingly anxious about its fate and about the lack of progress at Cassino, this was just not enough and Freyberg knew it. Despite Dimoline's reluctance to launch 4th Indian Division in a major attack without first securing Point 593, Freyberg insisted that the Indians attack Monte Cassino and the New Zealanders Cassino town on the night of 17/18 February. What had seemed so hopeful earlier in the month, as New Zealand Corps prepared to take over from II Corps, was now little more than desperation.

Desperation: 4th Indian Division on Monte Cassino, 2nd New Zealand Division at Cassino railway station.
The Indian Division's plan was ambitious. Rather than seizing each Point in turn along the Monte Cassino height leading to the monastery, Dimoline and the 7th Brigade commander, Brigadier Lovett, hoped to capture them in an attack on a broad 1,500-yard front using four battalions. There was by now plenty of experience indicating that success in such attacks depended upon

numbers of infantry, and being able to deploy them. This was an attempt to use as many as possible simultaneously, instead of allowing the German to repulse individual attacks on a restricted frontage. With the 1st Royal Sussex providing a firm base, the 4th/6th Rajputana Rifles would attack Point 593 at midnight on 17 February and, after capturing it, push on towards Point 444 below the west side of the monastery. With Point 593 hopefully captured, they would be followed at 0200 by the 1st/9th Gurkhas and, on their left, the 1st/2nd Gurkhas attacking Points 450, 444, and 445 to reach the monastery; thereafter two further battalions of 5th Indian Brigade would enter the north of Cassino town to assist the New Zealanders, who would have crossed the Rapido and broken into the town from the south-east.

The New Zealand Division's intention was to gain a bridgehead over the river and a foothold into the town as quickly as possible to enable armour to get across as the first stage of opening Highway 6. To minimise the risk of tanks bogging in the waterlogged ground, as the Americans had earlier experienced to the north of the town, the New Zealanders planned to use the railway embankment, some 30 feet wide, as their route. This ran into the town from the south-east to reach the railway station, a mile to the south of the town centre, but the Germans had deliberately breached it in twelve places over its last 1,000 yards. On the night of 17/18 February, troops of the 28th Maori Battalion were to move along the railway embankment to capture the station, while two companies of engineers filled the remaining eight breaches (the nearest four had already been filled), and throw bridges across the Rapido and its tributary. The plan was ambitious in that this was to be done by daylight, when the New Zealand 19th Armoured Regiment and anti-tank guns were to cross to support the Maoris. The Germans holding Cassino town would be contained, and a link-up made with the Indians pushing down from Monte Cassino.

Both the Indians and New Zealanders were to receive a heavy scale of fire support from the artilleries of New Zealand Corps and US II Corps, some 400 guns in all. For the Indians on the slopes, so close to the German positions, this could not be direct support, but would target German artillery positions and likely forming-up areas for counter-attack and reinforcement routes. That was all very well, but in this instance of the difficulty of providing artillery support in mountain fighting, it meant that the German positions immediately ahead of the Indian troops would not be neutralised by fire. Yet, it was precisely such positions in such terrain that could so quickly stop an attack. The Maoris attacking Cassino town would be more fortunate; a heavy ten-minute bombardment of their objective would precede their advance before lifting to engage deeper targets. The entire plan was very risky. On Monte Cassino, the Indian infantry were to be thrown against positions about which little was known except that they were formidable, in difficult ground that was also too little known. There had been no time for adequate reconnaissance, and all too many of the American soldiers who had fought over and knew the ground and might have helped were lying up there dead, or were in field hospitals. In Cassino town a single battalion, spearheaded by only two companies, was to be sent against a defence that had defied an American regiment, in the hope that the Americans had drawn the strength of the defences to the other side of the town, and that a route would be constructed in a single night over which tank support could reach them. The entire operation of New Zealand Corps was a gamble bearing alarming similarities to the infantry sacrifices of the Western Front, and Freyberg himself reckoned its chances as no more than 'fifty-fifty'.[18]

At midnight on 17 February, troops of the leading companies of the 4th/6th Rajputanas attacked Point 593, meeting machine-gun and mortar fire and grenades, as German flares burst overhead illuminating them. The Rajputanas pressed forward, making extensive use of grenades, and some broke into the German positions on the crest, where they died. The troops of the following companies were pinned by heavy cross-fire from nearby features and were unable to get forward. The Rajputanas retained a precarious hold on the slopes leading to their objective, and prepared to repel counter-attack. By dawn, the battalion had suffered 196 casualties. Shortly after 0200 the leading troops of 1st/9th Gurkhas attacked towards Point 444. Thrown off course by heavy machine-gun fire from positions on Points 593 and 569, those of 'A' Company in the lead headed for Point 450, while those of 'B' Company tried to clear Point 593, where the 4th/6th Rajputanas were already in trouble, and Point 569. The troops of either company made more than 300 yards in the face of the German fire, and those intended to follow them were pinned to their start lines. The attempt cost the 1st/9th Gurkhas 94 casualties.

The 1st/2nd Gurkhas attacked at 0330, directed upon Point 445 and the northern side of the monastery. The attack was on a two-company front, troops of 'C' and 'B' Companies leading. Their instructions were typical infiltration, they were to penetrate through a tract of scrub just ahead of their start line and advance as quickly as possible, bypassing points of resistance and leaving them to the troops of the companies intended to follow them. As they broke cover they were spotted in the moonlight and came under machine-gun cross-fire; they ran headlong into the scrub, and into disaster. Instead of providing cover, the scrub was a dense chest-high thicket of thorn, its edges sown with anti-personnel mines and extensively rigged with tripwire booby-traps. Farther in were unsuspected machine-gun positions 50 yards apart, between which individual paratroops were dug-in with machine-pistols and grenades. Most of the Gurkhas in the leading sections died as they entered the scrub, detonating the booby-traps and mines, and the bodies of several were later found with up to four trip wires coiled around their ankles. Those following them, despite great gallantry in trying to slash their way forward, could make no progress, and eventually went to ground. As dawn broke they were withdrawn to their start line; their battalion had lost eleven officers and 138 men. The other battalions had also fallen back to their start lines by now and although Brigadier Lovett suggested renewing the attack under smoke cover supported by a brigade of New Zealanders, Freyberg and Dimoline demurred. The 4th Indian Division had taken some 500 casualties in a few hours and, for the moment, enough was enough. It had been defeated as much by the ground as by the Germans. Nothing had been gained, and the German defenders holding the Monte Cassino positions, three battalions of paratroops and the Parachute MG Battalion, had suffered little.

On 17 and 18 February, the Maori Battalion crossed the Rapido by means of the railway embankment, and the New Zealand engineers worked hard to repair it for tanks. While the Maoris established a bridgehead, it proved a case of dawn coming just an hour too soon.[19] Beginning at 2130 on 17 February, 'A' and 'B' Companies of the 28th Maori Battalion began their advance along the railway embankment. They were delayed at first by the engineers' equipment, and nearer their objective they came under German mortar and machine-gun fire. By midnight, however, they occupied the railway station yards, having overcome several German positions. 'B' Company cleared the station, but could not reach its second objective, a group of buildings 200 yards to the north on the road into the town. 'A' Company was unable to capture some mounds to the south of the engine sheds called the 'Hummock', as it turned out to be a formidable position protected by a 20-foot-wide ditch full of water and covered by machine-guns.

For most of the night the New Zealand engineers worked under fire, the moonlight assisting the German observers on the high ground. By dawn the embankment still had two demolitions unbridged, preventing tanks from crossing. Engineer work had to cease with daylight bringing more accurate observed fire, but the two Maori companies were ordered to hold on in and around the station, under cover of smoke fired by artillery, until support could reach them. An attempt to reinforce the Maoris in daylight with more infantry would have risked heavy losses, but had it been tried, it might well have turned the scale at the station. As it was, the Maoris fought hard to hold on, but came under increasing fire and infiltrating attack by German troops of the Cassino garrison. These consisted of two battalions of the 211th Grenadier Regiment, the 3rd Battalion of the 361st Panzer Grenadier Regiment, an assault gun battery and several tanks.

By late afternoon the Maori companies, out of communication with their battalion headquarters, could hold out no longer, threatened by tanks and lacking anti-tank weapons, their PIAT ammunition all expended. The survivors pulled back across the Rapido; of the 200 who had first crossed, 22 had been killed, 78 wounded and 24 were missing. They had inflicted 9 killed, 102 wounded and 18 missing on the Germans, who were very glad to see them go. The German battalions had already been depleted in the heavy fighting against the US 34th Division and subjected for days to near continuous heavy artillery fire. They were combat-weary and their commanders knew that they were not up to the strain of a major battle, and that their units in the town lacked the strength to resist a further heavy New Zealand attack. When reporting their success to Kesselring, von Vietinghoff frankly admitted that he had not expected the Cassino garrison to retake the railway station from the New Zealanders; 'Neither did I,' replied Kesselring. The second battle of Cassino was over.[20]

Strategic Reappraisal: The Diadem Concept
On 20 February, two days after the end of the second battle of Cassino, the German attack on the Anzio beachhead petered out. After heavy fighting, and attacking with great determination and courage, the Germans broke off the battle. They had been unable to dislodge the British and American troops from their main defensive positions, and they had taken tremendous punishment from Allied artillery, naval gunfire and air attacks. Von Mackensen's infantry casualties in Fourteenth Army amounted to 5,389 men in four days' fighting, combat troops that could be ill-spared. Taking the offensive in Italy had brought no more luck to Kesselring than to Alexander. The troops of VI Corps at Anzio had won a significant defensive victory, and despite the sacrifice of the Indians and New Zealanders at the Gustav Line, they had won it alone.

With the beachhead now secure and spring weather on the way, however, Alexander sensed that Allied fortunes were set to change. Kesselring would soon lose his major ally, winter, and the Allies would be able to use their weight of air power with far greater effect, and the ground would be drying out for armour. Moreover, Kesselring had now shot his offensive bolt at Anzio, and his forces would be stretched trying to hold two major defensive fronts: to contain the beachhead and hold the Gustav Line. Alexander began to regard the beachhead as a firm base for a breakout offensive linked to a breakthrough of the Gustav Line. Lucas, as had become clear to Alexander and Clark, was not the man to lead a breakout from Anzio. He had also deeply frustrated Churchill, whose hopes for 'Shingle' had been so disappointed, and who had seen his 'wild cat' become a 'stranded whale'. The American General Lucian Truscott, who had commanded the US 3rd Infantry Division in the beachhead and whose grip on command of the Allied forces proved far stronger, replaced him. Lucas, the unhappy man who had failed to shake the Gustav Line in January, but whose emphasis upon a secure beachhead ultimately ensured the defeat of 'Fischfang', left his beachhead to his successor, and to future generations one of the most tantalising 'what-ifs' of military history.

The concept of linking a breakout from Anzio with a renewed offensive through the Gustav Line evolved through General John Harding, Alexander's Chief of Staff since January. Harding presciently identified the most effective way for the campaign in Italy to meet the requirement of the Allied Combined Chiefs of Staff of assisting 'Overlord'. This would be for Alexander's armies to compel Hitler to pour forces into Italy to avert disaster, not merely by pushing back the German line, but by destroying a large part of Kesselring's Army

Group.[21] The appreciation submitted by Alexander on 22 February to Wilson and to General Sir Alan Brooke, the Chief of the Imperial General Staff, reflected Harding's concept. It advocated a build-up in the Anzio beachhead of a force of up to four divisions for an offensive towards Valmontone, linked with a deep penetration through the Gustav Line and rapid advance into the Liri Valley. This would stand a good chance of cutting off and destroying a large proportion of the German Tenth Army opposing the main body of Fifth Army.[22] The concept was far more realistic than the original 'Shingle' plan. Whereas 'Shingle' was never more than a hurried gamble, Harding's concept, endorsed by Alexander, had solidity, and as it took firmer shape, it was code-named 'Diadem'.

The solidity and realism of 'Diadem' depended upon the meeting of several criteria, reflecting an assimilation of hard-won experience in Italy. One was that an offensive required sufficient superiority at the decisive point of attack, in effect a superiority of three-to-one in that essential commodity, infantry. The proposed build-up in the Anzio beachhead reflected this, but the principal challenge remained the Gustav Line, against which Fifth Army's attacks thus far had failed mainly through the lack of that vital infantry strength. Alexander's solution was radical. He would bring over the Apennines the main strength of Oliver Leese's Eighth Army, which would take responsibility for the Cassino sector and provide the striking force for the Liri Valley. This would bring a strength of some ten divisions in four corps; General Kirkman's British XIII Corps, General Anders' II Polish Corps, recently arrived in Italy, and General Burns' I Canadian Corps. McCreery's British X Corps would leave Clark's Fifth Army to come under Eighth Army command. In addition to running the breakout from Anzio, Fifth Army's emphasis would become an attack along the coastal route, Highway 7, by Keyes' II Corps. Juin's French Corps, still in Fifth Army, would take over the Garigliano sector to support Eighth Army's southern flank.[23]

This rationalisation of strength and reorganisation demanded an operational pause, and Alexander considered that it would be mid-April before he was ready to launch 'Diadem'. He also needed to be sure that the Allied Combined Chiefs would not denude him of the essential troops because of other operations to support 'Overlord', and particularly the proposed invasion of southern France – 'Anvil' – in the spring. In this, he received not only Churchill's support in winning over the initially reluctant American Joint Chiefs, but Eisenhower's crucial backing as well. Eisenhower needed no convincing of Alexander's difficulties. He too believed that a major offensive in Italy that would destroy significant German forces and draw even more would be the best means of supporting his cross-Channel invasion, and justified the temporary priority in the Mediterranean. On 26 February, the Allied Combined Chiefs assured Alexander of this, and while 'Anvil' would deprive him of forces in Italy after 'Overlord', 'Diadem' was on. Kesselring would remain capable of achieving significant tactical success for some weeks to come, but he was being set up for strategic defeat.

Two significant problems remained to confront Alexander. One was that his hands were still tied concerning the Liri Valley. He had no other possible route through which to exploit his superior armour and mobility in a drive to link up with the Anzio force to trap the Germans south of Rome. 'Diadem' depended upon the Liri Valley, and that still meant Cassino. While the Germans held the Cassino position, blocking Highway 6, they would prevent any such advance. However sound a concept, an outflanking move through the mountains was possible only by small forces dependent upon mule supply columns, of which there were never enough, and such forces remained vulnerable to counter-attack. It was not possible to sustain an army's advance through the mountains, and use of Highway 6 demanded the capture of Cassino as a preliminary for the success of 'Diadem'. The other problem was that, although an operational pause was necessary to regroup the armies for 'Diadem', Kesselring could not be allowed too much respite to regroup and rest his own forces, or to complete further defensive lines in the Liri Valley. He had to be kept under attack, and the soundest means of doing so would be to secure ground from which to launch 'Diadem' once the regrouping was complete and the weather favourable. Again, this meant Cassino, the capture of which would unlock Highway 6 and provide the bridgehead across the Rapido from which to burst into the Liri Valley. For these reasons, in late February 1944, Alexander was prepared to countenance another attempt by Freyberg's New Zealand Corps to capture Cassino by direct attack.

Freyberg's Second Attempt at Cassino: Operation 'Dickens'
Freyberg's own ideas had crystallised by the end of the second battle. He considered a wide envelopment of Cassino. The New Zealand Division might cross the Rapido to the south near San Angelo and break into the Liri Valley to link up with 4th Indian Division, which might carry out Tuker's proposed turning movement to the north of Monte Castellone. This he rejected. Too many dead American soldiers of Walker's 36th Division testified to the risks of crossing near San Angelo, and there appeared no satisfactory method of keeping 4th Indian sufficiently supplied in the mountains. Freyberg's focus remained on Cassino itself. He decided to attack the town from the north, as the strongest German defences covered the eastern approaches, where the river would also have to be bridged under observation from Monte Cassino and the monastery ruins. There were good road approaches into the town from the north, and the start line for an attack could be the ground already held on the northern outskirts by the US 133rd Infantry. To enable his infantry and tanks to break into the town and establish a firm foothold, Freyberg wanted the town pulverised by an unprecedented scale of air bombing and artillery fire immediately before the assault. This would destroy the German positions and their occupants, or at least render them incapable of reacting. The Indian Division would support and protect the New Zealanders' right flank by attacking across

> **GERMAN 1ST PARACHUTE DIVISION**
> (Major-General Richard Heidrich) Cassino, March–May 1944[24]
>
> | | |
> |---|---|
> | Cassino Town | 2nd/3rd Parachute Regiment |
> | South of Cassino/Railway Station | Parachute MG Bn |
> | Monte Cassino/Castle Hill (Point 193) | 1st/3rd Parachute Regiment |
> | Colle San Angelo/Point 593 | 4th Parachute Regiment (three battalions) |
> | Colle San Angelo – Monte Cairo | 1st Parachute Regiment (two battalions) |
>
> 1st Parachute Division combat strength (Cassino sector 14 March 1944): approximately 6,000 men.
>
> **Firepower:**
> 1 x battery 10cm parachute artillery
> 1 x battery 7.5cm mountain guns
> 2 x batteries medium artillery
> 2 x batteries light artillery
> 13 Italian-built assault guns (Semovente)
> 28 medium anti-tank guns (8 self-propelled)
> Plus 71st Werfer Regiment of mixed 15cm six-barrelled Nebelwerfer rocket launchers and 21cm five-barrelled Nebelwerfer rocket launchers, to a total of 88 barrels.

Monte Cassino to secure Point 236 and Point 435 – 'Hangman's Hill' – and then the monastery.

On 19 February, at a meeting with Clark, Alexander, and Wilson, who was on a visit to the Italian battlefront, the plan was accepted. Alexander ordered that three dry days must precede the attack to ensure the use of tanks, and that the attack would open on a day of clear visibility for the bombers. The senior Allied airmen later agreed their full support, but held mixed views. Major General John Cannon commanding the Mediterranean Allied Tactical Air Force enthusiastically believed that the bombing would succeed in blasting a way through for the troops, Eaker was less sanguine. His knowledge of what the heavy strategic bombers could do to a town was probably greater, and he warned Freyberg that the resulting rubble would impede his troops and especially his tanks. Freyberg's view was that this would be a problem for the Germans too, and that besides he could use bulldozers to clear routes. Eaker remained convinced about none of this, except possibly that when it came to heavy bombing the soldiers did not know what they were talking about, but promised full support when the weather allowed. In fact a period of rain, bitter cold winds, sleet and snow began on 23 February, a harsh reminder that winter was not yet over. It persisted until 14 March, much to the misery of the troops on both sides, but especially those on the mountain slopes.

During this lull, the Germans carried out their own regrouping at Cassino. Major-General Richard Heidrich's 1st Parachute Division took over full responsibility for the Cassino position, finally relieving all other units in and around the town, including those of Baade's 90th Panzer Grenadier Division. Heidrich and his staff were now determined to make the defence of Cassino a Luftwaffe all-paratroop affair, and his men busied themselves by strengthening further the cellar and bunker positions in Cassino town.

In the same period the 6th New Zealand Infantry Brigade took over the positions of the US 133rd Infantry on the northern edge of the town. They found themselves overlooked by Point 193 (Castle Hill), and peering across the width of streets at what they knew to be strong German positions.

'Dickens' was dependent upon a formidable weight of firepower. In addition to heavy bombers, there would be medium and light bombers and, providing they were not required at Anzio, fighter-bombers as well. A Forward Air Controller at New Zealand Division's tactical headquarters stood by to direct the fighter-bombers' attacks. The New Zealanders reckoned that, if there were a thousand German troops in Cassino town, three 1,000lb bombs would drop for each of them.[25] There were also some 900 guns of the combined British, New Zealand, American and even French artilleries in range, and 250,000 rounds stockpiled.

On the morning of the attack the bombers and artillery were to saturate Cassino with fire. Then, at noon, the troops of 6th New Zealand Brigade supported by tanks of the 19th Armoured Regiment would advance into the town under cover of a creeping artillery barrage at a rate of 100 yards in ten minutes. By 1400 they were to have taken 'Castle Hill' and cleared the town as far as Highway 6. This was optimistic, suggesting a confident belief that at least one of the three bombs allotted to each German in the town would be sure to find its mark. There also appears to have been far too little consideration given to Eaker's rubble. The 7th Indian Brigade, holding 4th Indian Division's front, would support by taking German positions, especially 'Castle Hill' under fire. The 5th Indian Brigade would follow up the New Zealanders, taking over 'Castle Hill'. The New Zealanders would push on through the town to clear the railway station and the 'Hummock' to the south, while troops of 5th Indian Brigade attacked across the eastern slopes of Monte Cassino to capture Point 435 ('Hangman's Hill'). Given the Indian Division's earlier experience of attacking across this terrain, this part of the plan also seems unduly optimistic. However, there was an audacious intention to introduce tanks into the battle in this sector. They were to make a thrust in the form of a hook along 'Cavendish Road', a track ascending for 800 feet over a mile and a half from Cairo village to Colle Majola in a gradient of one in four. In early March, Indian and New Zealand engineers worked hard to widen this for tanks. A mixed armoured force composed of sixteen Shermans of the 20th New Zealand Armoured Regiment, sixteen Stuart light tanks of the US 760th Tank Battalion, and three Shermans and five Stuarts of the Indian Division's Reconnaissance Squadron were to advance along this route towards Point 593 and the Albaneta Farm, then turn south-east along Monte Cassino in the direction of the monastery. Even with 'Cavendish Road' widened, the ground would remain extremely difficult and the tanks, unable to manoeuvre, would be vulnerable. Much would depend upon their shock and surprise effect on German troops who would never expect to be threatened by armour from that direction or over such ground. The idea bears striking resemblance to the earlier American attempt to introduce armour into their battle for San Pietro, and the imperative was just as desperate. Such was the plan, and on 14 March, with a forecast for good weather on the next day, New Zealand Corps decided that 'Dickens' was on. The forward troops in Cassino pulled back in anticipation of the bombing.

Street Fighting: Cassino
From 0830 until noon, with intervals of about a quarter of an hour, over 400 heavy and medium bombers dropped just over a thousand tons of bombs on Cassino. The bombing was reasonably accurate for its time, with just under fifty per cent of the bombs bursting within a mile of the town centre. As they departed, the guns poured shells into the smoking rubble. The town became an inferno, in which many paratroops died. Of the 300 or so paratroops in the 2nd Battalion, at least 160 were buried under the rubble, along with four of its five assault guns.[26] The survivors, however, emerged from the strong shelters that had protected them, dug themselves out of the rubble, and prepared to defend – these were no ordinary soldiers. As the leading companies of the 25th New Zealand Battalion and their supporting Shermans entered the north of the town they came under immediate fire. The New Zealand infantry struggled forward to locate and destroy the German positions with grenades, but found themselves fighting in a disorienting crazy maze of craters and rubble. Instead of 100 yards in ten minutes they were lucky to cover that distance in an hour. Where they could, the tanks engaged suspected German positions with 75mm fire at near point-blank range, but they could not get forward because of the huge piles of masonry thrown down by the bombing, which even desperate attempts at ramming could not budge. As daylight faded, the infantry had taken 'Castle Hill' and were within reach of Highway 6, but most of their supporting tank regiment was still waiting to enter the town from the north, blocking the roads for the engineer companies that alone could get them forward. Then it began to rain. Huge bomb craters that might have been filled in instead became deep ponds requiring bridging equipment, and under the cover of dark the paratroops emerged to infiltrate back into the positions the New Zealanders thought were cleared. In the dark, the 26th New Zealand battalion attempted to enter the town, intending to pass through to attack the railway station area, but could make no progress in the confusion and had to await daylight.

In the early hours of 16 March, the 1st/4th Essex of 5th Indian Brigade occupied 'Castle Hill' and captured Point 165, after numerous and confusing short engagements with paratroops. The lead companies of the 1st/6th Rajputana

THE SECOND AND THIRD BATTLES OF CASSINO

Rifles attempted to take Point 236, but were held by German fire. The 1st/9th Gurkha Rifles, after a long march from Cairo village, reached the north of the town but could not find the other battalions. Their officers led them towards their objective, 'Hangman's Hill', but with the approach of daylight and the risk of exposure to German fire no attack was made – or so it was thought. In fact one company in two parties had ascended to the top of 'Hangman's Hill' after destroying a single German position with grenades. There they consolidated, and no one, Allied or German, knew they were there.

The following day saw a street-fighting battle of great confusion, led by the junior officers and NCOs on both sides as both the New Zealand Corps and German higher headquarters received only intermittent contact with their forces embroiled in the town. The New Zealanders struggled to solve the vicious circle of tanks being unable to get forward without bulldozers clearing a route, which they could not do without tank support because of short-range enemy fire. German positions were overcome one by one in a slow house-by-house and street-by-street attack, the New Zealanders often finding that the Germans had infiltrated through tunnels and houses to re-emerge behind them. Troops of

THE THIRD BATTLE OF MONTE CASSINO, 15–25 MARCH 1944: NZ Corps attempts to clear Cassino ('Dickens')

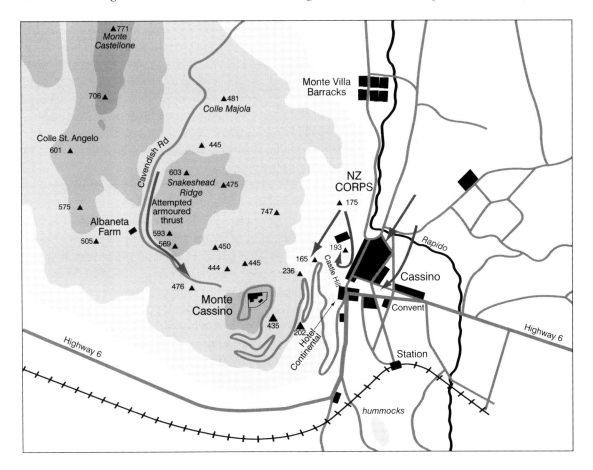

the 25th and 24th Battalions fought to clear the area and captured the convent south of Highway 6 supported by several Shermans that had entered the town from the east across a bridge over the Rapido erected by US engineers. News of the single Gurkha company on 'Hangman's Hill' prompted efforts to reinforce them, and the rest of their battalion reached them after a difficult climb early on 17 March. During the fighting on that day companies of the New Zealand 24th and 25th Battalions fought their way to within 200 yards of a major German stronghold, the Continental Hotel. The 26th Battalion entered the battle and with Shermans in support fought its way south and captured the railway station.

The paratroops' hold on the western edge of the town proved unbreakable, despite the New Zealanders fighting their way forward from one pile of rubble to the next, winkling out paratroop snipers in ones and twos, and their tanks blasting the houses and buildings section by section. When the pressure became too much the paratroops would pull back, to set up their positions in the next building or street. At night, they filtered in reinforcements and supplies, and used the myriad tunnels and cellars to redeploy. This made the problems of clearing areas of the town and mopping-up immensely difficult and frustrating for the New Zealanders. In a typical example, an intrepid German paratrooper suddenly emerged from a pile of rubble in an area twenty-four hours after it was cleared, and managed to set fire to a tank. On another occasion, the New Zealand infantry cleared one sector in some difficult night fighting, yet still had to winkle out another hundred or so paratroops from it later.[27] The 5th Indian Brigade had difficulty in getting supplies to its own troops on both 'Castle Hill' and 'Hangman's Hill'. Porters, at great risk, reached both, but the approaches to 'Hangman's Hill' proved too exposed to German fire and aggressive patrolling, so between 18 and 24 March Mustang fighter-bombers made nearly 200 sorties that kept the Gurkhas supplied with food, water and ammunition, but only just. On 19 March the battle reached a higher pitch of intensity as both sides sought decisive success. A composite force of the 1st and 4th Rajputana Rifles was intended to relieve the 1st/4th Essex on 'Castle Hill' and Point 165, enabling the Essex to join the Gurkhas on 'Hangman's Hill' for an attack on the monastery combined with the armoured thrust from 'Cavendish Road'. The relief was interrupted by Heidrich, who launched a ferocious counter-attack to recapture 'Castle Hill' with the 1st/4th Parachute Regiment. In a fierce and prolonged battle of machine-gun fire and showers of grenades, the paratroops fought to break into the castle ruins, much as their medieval predecessors would have done, by scaling the walls and undermining the battlements. They tried repeatedly, with heavy losses and without success. By the time the garrison of about 150 Essex and Indian troops finally repulsed them, no Essex officers on 'Castle Hill' remained alive unwounded. At the height of the fighting, a paratrooper NCO earlier taken prisoner stalked about in the open as if critically observing the conduct of the battle, afterwards complimenting the senior surviving Essex officer on his defence, and presenting him with his paratrooper's gauntlets as souvenirs. It was a professional military theatricality typifying the *esprit de corps* of Heidrich's men.[28]

Of the two Essex companies sent to 'Hangman's Hill', only about 70 men arrived. The tank attack along 'Cavendish Road' reached as far as the Albaneta Farm and, according to intercepted signals, caused the Germans some initial consternation. Against less determined troops it might have succeeded, but the paratroops kept their nerve and covered the tanks with small-arms fire, reducing further the already limited visibility of their crews. Anti-tank grenades disabled several. Without infantry, who could not have braved the heavy German fire, the tanks were helpless and their attack soon stalled.

Freyberg was under some pressure from Clark to put more infantry into the town, but this he resisted believing there to be more than enough in a confined battle area. Nevertheless, on 19 March he decided to feed in further New Zealand infantry of 5th Brigade, and units of the British 78th Division, the 6th Royal West Kents, to take over 'Castle Hill' from the Essex. For three more days the battle continued without significant gain for either side, the New Zealanders unable to take the town completely, and Heidrich's paratroops unable to eject them from it. The monastery remained beyond the hopes of the exhausted 5th Indian Brigade. At a meeting with Alexander, Clark and Leese on 21 March, Freyberg argued for a few days more to continue the attack. Alexander, unwilling to compromise 'Diadem' by heavy losses, nevertheless allowed himself to be persuaded. Two days later Freyberg himself advised Clark that the battle should be ended, and Clark agreed. So did Alexander, at the front to see for himself and reportedly uttering the one word 'Passchendaele'.[29] During the night of 24/25 March, the gallant Gurkhas on 'Hangman's Hill' quietly withdrew, as did the New Zealanders of the 24th Battalion who were on Point 202. The third battle of Cassino was over.[30]

Heidrich and his paratroops had won a defensive battle of which they could be justifiably proud. In a signal to Churchill Alexander himself remarked on their tenacity despite the weight of firepower thrown at them, adding that 'I doubt if there are any other troops in the world who could have stood up to it and then gone on fighting with the ferocity they have.'[31] For all that, the soldiers of the New Zealand and Indian Divisions had dealt very severely with them. They had reduced Heidrich's battalions to strengths of between 40 and 120 men, and like the Americans and French before them, they had given von Senger and von Vietinghoff good cause to worry. Just how close they came to success is hard to determine. As with the earlier battles of the Gustav Line, the German defence was undoubtedly pushed to breaking point, but the attacking strength was never quite enough to make it snap. It will always remain debatable whether an earlier commitment of more infantry into the battle, albeit with the consequent acceptance of higher casualties, would have clinched success. As it was, the casualties of New Zealand Corps were reckoned at 287 killed, 1,582 wounded, and 237 missing, bad enough, but not Passchendaele.[32]

At the height of the battle on 20 March, Alexander received an anxious signal from Churchill. 'I wish you would explain to me,' he demanded, 'why this passage by Cassino, Monastery Hill, etc., all on a front of 2 or 3 miles is the only place you must keep butting at. About 5 or 6 divisions have been worn out going into these jaws.' It was an impatient, inevitable and not unreasonable demand from the Italian Campaign's principal advocate, who wanted to know why the Cassino position could not be outflanked. 'Along the whole of the main battle front from the Adriatic to the South coast,' replied Alexander, 'there is only the Liri Valley leading direct to Rome which is suitable terrain for the deployment of our superiority in artillery and armour. The main highway known as route six is the only road except cart tracks which leads from the mountains where we are into the Liri Valley over the Rapido River and this exit into the plain is blocked and dominated by Monte Cassino on which stands the Monastery.' It was as simple as that. Without making considerably more effort to infiltrate through the mountains, there was no choice. Juin's troops had at least demonstrated the potential of such a move, and Tuker of the 4th Indian Division had favoured it. The undoubted risks involved, however, were always likely to have been too much for the commanders of the mechanised and road-dependent Anglo-American armies to accept, especially when one more push at Cassino might unlock the Liri Valley. In his reply to Churchill, Alexander added that as soon as the regrouping of his forces was complete, he would carry out the plan for Eighth Army to enter the Liri Valley in force.[33]

6

MONTE CASSINO: A POLISH BATTLE

Freyberg's New Zealand Corps disbanded on 26 March, its sector taken over by the XIII Corps of Eighth Army. The ground hard-won during 'Dickens', positions running from 'Castle Hill' through the town to the railway station and the 'Hummock', were taken over in early April by the 1st Guards Brigade. They consolidated firmly, with mines laid and wire strung to contain their troublesome neighbours of Heidrich's Parachute Division and prevent their infiltrating. The 78th Division relieved the long-suffering 4th Indian Division on 'Snakeshead Ridge' and the slopes above the town, amid the rotting corpses of American, Indian and German soldiers whose removal for proper burial proved impossible to risk under fire. The troops of 78th Division, including Fred Majdalany, a company commander in 2nd Lancashire Fusiliers and later a historian of the Cassino battles, held these positions under the grim walls of the monastery until the end of April. Then, troops arrived to relieve them whose keenness to get to grips with the Germans bordered on the foolhardy.[1] Fresh troops with scores to settle, whose country was suffering the worst excesses of Nazi occupation: the Poles. Theirs was to be the next and final battle of Cassino.

'Strangle'

As Alexander regrouped his forces for 'Diadem', Kesselring's armies were already under heavy attack, from the air. Beginning on 19 March, the Allied heavy, medium and fighter-bombers began systematic attacks on the rail and road communications in Italy upon which Kesselring's armies depended for their supplies. This interdiction operation, code-named 'Strangle', aimed to disrupt supply traffic to the extent that the Tenth and Fourteenth Armies would be unable to maintain their operations against Alexander's offensive. Fighter-bombers of the two Allied tactical air forces, the US XII Air Support Command usually supporting Fifth Army and RAF Desert Air Force supporting Eighth Army, flew some 22,000 sorties, mainly against road movement. The heavy and medium bombers attacked railway marshalling yards, bridges, tunnels and stretches of track in an attempt to paralyse railway communications along their full length from northern Italy to the battlefront. Ports were also heavily bombed. Originally the 'Strangle' concept intended such paralysis of German communications in Italy that their armies would have been compelled to withdraw without a major ground offensive. This was excessively optimistic, and although some senior airmen had such optimism and enthused General Sir Henry Maitland Wilson with the concept, Alexander remained unconvinced, and he was right. The Germans had stockpiled supplies near their front-line positions, moved supplies by night, and enough always trickled through. Their shortages before 'Diadem' never became critical. Nevertheless the air campaign, which ultimately involved over 50,000 sorties, caused depletion of their stockpiles and reduced their ability to sustain prolonged battle. They also suffered heavy losses in motor transport when attempting movement in daylight and their redeployment and manoeuvre became harder.[2] For the first time, Kesselring's forces felt the full weight of Allied air power directed against them throughout the length of Italy. It was the first of the indications to arrive with the improved weather that the fortunes of the campaign were shifting in Allied favour.

'Diadem'

Throughout April, Alexander's armies received significant reinforcement, bringing his strength to twenty-five divisions. Two new US Infantry Divisions, the 88th and 85th arrived to join Keyes' II Corps in Fifth Army, enabling the 34th to go to Anzio and the 36th into Clark's reserve. Juin's French Corps received the 4th Moroccan Mountain Division, and the 1st Free French Infantry Division, bringing his strength to four divisions in addition to his force of irregular Goums. Eighth Army received the 10th Indian Division and the 6th South African Armoured Division, and the British 4th Infantry and 6th Armoured Divisions, enabling a relief of the weary 46th and 56th Divisions. In great secrecy, and without alerting the Germans to the full extent of the regrouping, the Allied formations took up their positions for 'Diadem'. The British V Corps covered the Adriatic sector with the 10th Indian and battle-worn 4th Indian Divisions, directly under Alexander's Headquarters to relieve Eighth Army of their administration. The X Corps, with the New Zealand Division and several brigades, took over the mountain positions either side of the Apennines, while the II Polish Corps moved in on the right of XIII Corps in preparation for taking over the Cassino sector. Opposite the Liri Valley and Highway 6 was XIII Corps, with the 8th Indian, the British 4th and 78th Infantry Divisions and the 6th Armoured Division. Here, with General Kirkman's XIII Corps, Alexander and Leese intended to burst into the Liri Valley with the sheer weight of numbers that Fifth Army had never had. In reserve waiting to exploit was the I Canadian Corps, with the 1st Canadian Division, the 5th Canadian Armoured Division and a tank brigade. To the south was Clark's Fifth Army, with Juin's Corps waiting to break into the Aurunci Mountains and Keyes ready to move up Highway 7 along the coast.

Alexander's intention was to destroy the right wing of the Tenth Army, and drive its remnant and that of Four-

Right: On the receiving end: bombs exploding amidst German positions on Point 476 on the high ground near Cassino during an Allied bombardment in April 1944, a German photograph taken from a safe distance using a camera fitted with a telescopic lens. In the background is the Liri Valley and Highway 6, indicating the excellent observation accorded the Germans by possession of the heights around Cassino.

teenth Army to the north of Rome as far as a line between Pisa and Rimini. The overriding aim was not to get to Rome, but to cut off and destroy as many of the German divisions as possible. Eighth Army was to break through to the Liri Valley along Highway 6 to the east of Rome, while Fifth Army would make a parallel advance in the south. At a time ordered by Alexander, Truscott would launch his breakout from Anzio and move east to cut Highway 6 in the area of Valmontone,

Below: Polish troops photographed moving up to their start line on Monte Cassino in the dusk. Their casualties in the ensuing battle were very heavy.

thereby cutting off the retreat of much of von Vietinghhoff's Tenth Army. Clark insisted, however, that Truscott also prepare plans for striking in the direction of Rome. Although 'Diadem' envisaged Fifth Army entering Rome, Clark was not prepared to risk Eighth Army reaching the Italian capital first. That was an honour he felt belonged to his Fifth Army that had well earned it. He suspected that Eighth Army, reflecting British interests in a British-dominated theatre, might usurp it.[3]

Although the Germans detected evidence of a major Allied regrouping, Kesselring could obtain no reliable intelligence as to the exact location of formations or any indication of when a renewed offensive, which he knew must come, would begin. The Allies had a comprehensive picture of his redeployments, however, through Enigma signals intelligence. This revealed that after the middle of April Kesselring, like Alexander, had placed only a holding force on the Adriatic sector. He had recognised that the Liri Valley sector and the approaches to Rome, and the Anzio front, would be the critical areas. Guarding the Adriatic flank was a new formation, Corps Group Hauck, based mainly upon the 305th and 324th Infantry Divisions. From the boundaries of this group, and extending to the Liri, including the Cassino sector, was the LI Mountain Corps, with the 44th Infantry, 1st Parachute, 5th Mountain, and 114th Jäger Divisions. From the Liri to Terracina on the coast, opposite Fifth Army, was von Senger's XIV Panzer Corps, with the 15th Panzer Grenadier, and the 94th and 71st Infantry Divisions.

The Allies also learned, from a signal intercepted on 28 April, that Kesselring had a total of 403 tanks in Italy, of which 310 were serviceable, including 197 with Fourteenth Army and only 37 with Tenth Army.[4] This was very few to set against the number possessed by the Allies in Italy, whose total of medium tanks alone was now some 3,000[5]. It was not just a question of numbers, however, but also of how the Germans might use the tanks that they did have.

Although the Allies were aware through signals intelligence and aerial reconnaissance that the Germans were constructing a number of fall-back defensive positions behind the Gustav Line, they were confident that Kesselring was not the commander to retreat before he was attacked. If they could achieve surprise in their breakthrough, the momentum of their advance through the Liri Valley might render these fall-back positions untenable. The period before 'Diadem', which Alexander decided would begin on 11 May, saw an elaborate deception plan put in motion. While the build-up opposite the Liri Valley was masked, the use of false signals traffic and an ostentatious concentration of shipping and amphibious exercises off Salerno successfully convinced Kesselring of the likelihood of another Allied seaborne amphibious landing on the west coast, this time at Civitavecchia north-west of Rome, and that an Allied offensive would not begin until the end of May. His forces were fully stretched to seal the Anzio beachhead and provide some reserve against a further landing, with his mobile forces deployed accordingly: the 29th Panzer Grenadier Division north of Rome and the 90th Panzer Grenadier and 26th Panzer Divisions between Anzio and the capital. In January, the Allies had deliberately induced Kesselring to send his mobile reserves south to the Gustav Line to make way for 'Shingle'. This had been a mistaken decision on Kesselring's part and an experience the Allies hoped would this time decide him to keep them where they were. When 'Diadem' broke on 11 May, the only German reserve near the Gustav Line was the 15th Panzer Grenadier Division. Weakened by heavy fighting, it still had two battalions along the Rapido. The Gustav Line had never been thinner. Believing that no Allied attack was likely to take place before 24 May, both von Senger of XIV Panzer Corps and von Vietinghoff were absent on leave. Just before 2300 on 11 May, Allied monitors of German wireless traffic picked up a voice from the monastery on Monte Cassino which said 'I am going down to the cemetery.' To the listeners, it seemed highly appropriate, for two minutes later the 1,060 guns of Eighth Army and the 600 of Fifth Army began their opening bombardment of 'Diadem.'[6]

It was Juin's French Corps that unhinged the Gustav Line. The German 71st Infantry Division offered initial resistance, later supported by a battalion of the 15th Panzer Grenadiers, but French momentum was such that the Germans had little time, and too little strength, to stop them. By the afternoon of 13 May the 2nd Moroccan Division was on Monte Majo, and by midnight the west bank of the Garigliano had been cleared to the junction of the Liri. On Juin's left, the 4th Moroccan Mountain Division secured the objectives that had remained out of reach to McCreery's British X Corps in January and early February; Castelforte

and Monte Damiano. Juin, with the door to the River Ausente Valley open, prepared to exploit to Ausonia and the Petrella Massif; the left front of the XIV Panzer Corps was broken, forcing a withdrawal also on its right along the coast. In this sector, Keyes' II Corps had made little progress. The US 85th and 88th Divisions, gaining their first combat experience, were held by the 94th Division's positions and by sharp counter-attacks, but late on 14 May the advance of the French compelled the Germans to fall back. By 17 May the Americans had taken Formia on the coast and were pushing towards Itri; two days later they had captured Monte Grande, turning the German coastal flank.

The British XIII Corps broke into the Liri Valley, after establishing a bridgehead over the Rapido on either side of San Angelo. Both the Corps commander, Kirkman, and Leese agreed that a crossing where the US 36th Division had met disaster would still be a better prospect that an attempt through ruined Cassino itself. They were in no mind to compromise the advance by a street-battle such as the New Zealanders had experienced, and at San Angelo they would have surprise – and more troops to clinch the battle than the unfortunate Walker. However, in the early stages of the attempt, on 12 May, history seemed to be repeating itself. The assault battalions of the British 4th Division took heavy losses in achieving a very narrow bridgehead under German fire, one battalion, the 6th East Surreys, taking 142 casualties. The other assault division, 8th Indian, also

Opposite page: Alexander's final co-ordinating conference for 'Diadem', held on 1 May 1944. Among those present were, left to right, General Harding, Alexander's Chief of Staff; General Leese commanding Eighth Army; General Lemnitzer, Alexander's American Deputy Chief of Staff; Field-Marshal Alexander; General Mark Clark commanding Fifth Army.

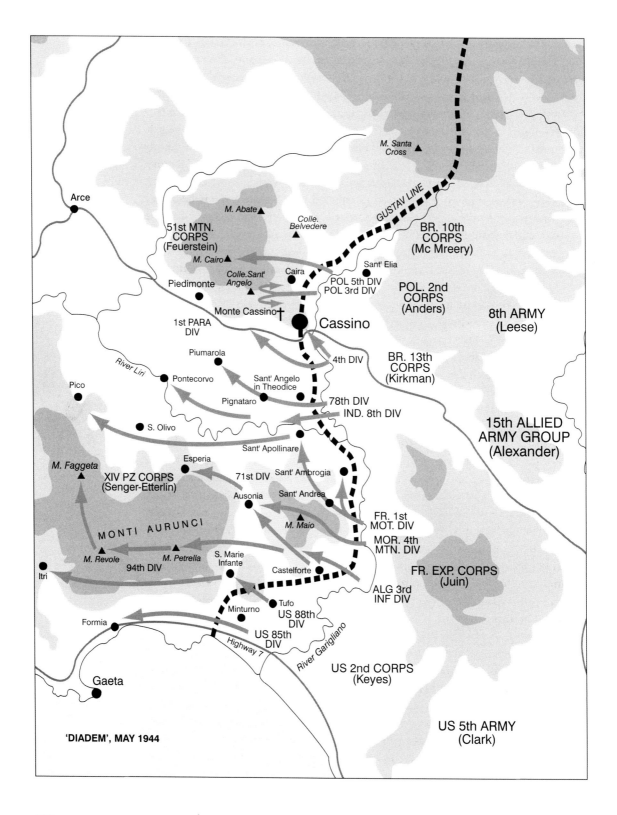

only secured a precarious foothold. Firepower and the work of the engineers turned the scale in this sector; two 30-ton Bailey bridges, one of them carried into the water by a Sherman tank, were erected, enabling Canadian tanks to cross. Their support, and a massive artillery barrage, enabled the 1/5th Gurkhas to take San Angelo on 13 May after several hours of savage street fighting that cost them 170 casualties. By now, the battalions in the bridgehead were starting to take significant numbers of prisoners; more than 400 by 4th Division, including some of Heidrich's 1st Paratroop Division, a counter-attack by whose Machine Gun Battalion the 4th Division shattered with heavy losses. The 8th Indian Division broke up counter-attacks by a battalion of the 15th Panzer Grenadier Division that were made in company strength. These were indications that the strength and co-ordination of the defence, and the morale of the German troops, were starting to break down.

Late on 13 May, Kirkman decided that the 78th Division with a reinforced armoured brigade would cross the river and continue the advance. Eighth Army had at last reached the ground denied the Allies for so long beyond the mountains. It was still good defender's country, however, undulating grassland with trees and hedges, ditches and walls. The infantry and supporting tanks of 78th Division had a difficult advance, overcoming well-constructed emplacements and resisting the usual sharp counter-attacks which at times were supported by a few tanks. Now, however, while there were stubborn points of resistance, the defence was crumbling, and by daylight the German troops were exposed to attack by the squadrons of fighter-bombers constantly overhead. By 17 May, the 78th Division had passed Pignataro and were closing to a German fall-back line, the Senger Line, known to the Allies as the Hitler Line. The 4th Division had reached Highway 6, and Canadian troops of I Canadian Corps began to pass through 8th Indian Division. The Canadian tanks and infantry also had some stiff fighting and heavy casualties against anti-tank ambushes in the Liri Valley, but by 19 May they had reached Pontecorvo, and Leese was planning his breakthrough of the Hitler Line. One of the most exhilarating experiences of this hard-fought advance for the British and Canadian troops was that they now had to look behind them to see Monte Cassino, but from 12 to 18 May it was shrouded from their view by the smoke of the battle raging there, as the Poles fought their own battle of Cassino.

General Anders' Battle
The Polish battle of Cassino would be one of great ferocity. As a subsequent report by the II Polish Corps noted, the German resistance to their attacks was desperate. In the main, German troops fought to the very end rather than surrender, and the Poles afterwards discovered that that this was at least partly due to a rumour widely spread among the Germans that the Poles would not be taking any prisoners.[7] This was not the case, but for their part, the Poles launched their attacks upon Monte Cassino with a stubbornness and tenacity

that reflected their determination to succeed for the sake of their tragic country. It was a dubious honour to be given the toughest proposition of 'Diadem', the capture of Monte Cassino, but when Leese had asked the Polish Corps commander, General Wladyslaw Anders, whether he was willing to tackle the

task, Anders agreed. He, his men, and their families had endured a harsh Soviet imprisonment following the partition of their country by Hitler and Stalin in 1939. With Hitler's invasion of the Soviet Union in 1941, Allied pressure had induced the reluctant Soviets to release the Poles, and they had made a difficult

journey across half of Europe to reach the Middle East. There, the British equipped them. Anders and his men wanted not only to deal the Germans a serious blow but also to demonstrate to the world that a free Polish Army existed and was fighting for its country. To take Monte Cassino would do both.

In military terms, by engaging and capturing the German positions on Monte Cassino, the Poles would prevent Heidrich's troops and observers from dominating the British XIII Corps crossing. They would also deny them the deep long-range observation of Eighth Army's dispositions and communications, and render untenable the German defensive positions opposite the British in the valley below. In fact, the Poles would place the Germans in the same predicament under the eyes of Monte Cassino and the monastery that the Allies had endured for months. The Poles were to hold this ground overlooking Highway 6 until a link-up could be made with XIII Corps. Unlike the Americans and Indians before them, the Polish Corps had more troops for the task, but it remained formidable and daunting. Heidrich's own forces had been thinned out since his battle with the New Zealanders. His regiments were each reduced to two weak battalions averaging 200–300 men, though his anti-tank and artillery firepower was increased, including a section of assault guns and one of 'Hornets', self-propelled 88mm guns on a Panzer Mk. III chassis.[8]

Anders received information from the New Zealanders and Indians about the formidable in-depth German defences of Monte Cassino and the ground, as they attempted to give the fruits of their bitter experience to the Poles. Anders, however, had no intention of

Opposite page: On the left is General Anders commanding II Polish Corps, in the centre is General Juin, commanding the French Expeditionary Corps, on the right is General Kirkman commanding the British XIII Corps.

109

Opposite page: A British soldier with his Bren light machine gun photographed amid the rubble of a ruined building in Cassino town on 18 May 1944. The thickness of the walls and the extent of the debris caused by artillery bombardment of the town provided excellent defensive positions to the German defenders who in February and March defied attacks by the US 34th Division and later by the New Zealand Corps.

GERMAN 1ST PARACHUTE DIVISION, DISPOSITIONS, CASSINO SECTOR, MAY 1944

Cassino Town and Monte Cassino: 4th Parachute Regiment (Parachute MG Bn under command)
Points 593–569 to Albaneta area: 1st/3rd Parachute Regiment
Area north-west of Colle San Angelo: 2nd/3rd Parachute Regiment
Colle San Angelo to Point 706 – Monte Castellone Sector: Battle Group von Ruffin (4th Independent Alpine Battalion and 2nd/100th Mountain Regiment of 5th Mountain Division)
Reserve (Villa Santa Lucia area): 1st Parachute Regiment reinforced by 2nd/721st Grenadier Regiment and 2nd/741st Grenadier Regiment (both of 114th Jäger Division)

---

trying to squeeze his men through the ruins of the town, or to repeat the Indian attacks on a narrow front along Monte Cassino from Colle Majola under German cross-fire from adjacent peaks. His plan was an amplification, with stronger forces, of that attempted by the US 34th Division in January. His 5th Kresowa Division would advance along the Monte Castellone feature to capture Colle San Angelo and Points 575, 505, 452 and 447 overlooking Highway 6 and the Liri Valley. The 3rd Carpathian Division would attack and capture Albaneta and the high ground Point 593 and Point 569, in preparation for an assault upon the monastery position that would, by then, be isolated.[9]

The Poles were to receive the direct fire support of nearly 300 guns, and Eighth Army provided 72 4.2in mortars, but not their crews, camouflage sniper suits and special picks for breaking the rocky ground. Other formations provided flame-throwers with which to subdue German positions. It seemed that every-

---

II POLISH CORPS (BRITISH EIGHTH ARMY), MAY 1944[10]
General W. Anders

3rd Carpathian Division (Major-General Duch)
1st Carpathian Rifle Brigade: 1st, 2nd, 3rd Carpathian Rifle Battalions
2nd Carpathian Rifle Brigade: 4th, 5th, 6th Carpathian Rifle Battalions
12th Podolski Lancers (Recce Regiment)
3rd Carpathian MG Bn.
Plus Divisional artillery and engineers.

5th Kresowa Division (Major-General Sulik)
5th Wilenski Infantry Brigade: 13th, 14th, 15th Wilenska Rifle Battalions
6th Lwowska Infantry Brigade: 16th, 17th Lwowska Rifle Battalions
15 Poznanski Regiment (Recce)
5th Kresowa MG Bn
Plus Divisional artillery and engineers.

2nd Polish Armoured Brigade: 1st Polish Armoured Cavalry, 4th Polish Armoured, 6th Lwowska Armoured Regiments.

Corps troops included two field and two medium artillery regiments, anti-tank and AA regiments and engineers, and an armoured car regiment (3rd Carpathian Lancers)

one wanted to help, but no one envied, the Poles. Like the Indians before them, however, they suffered one serious handicap. The Polish troops had no opportunity to closely reconnoitre the ground for themselves, in this case mainly because patrols were not carried out that would risk the Germans discovering that the Polish Corps was in the line.

At 0130 on 12 May the 1st and 2nd Carpathian Battalions followed the artillery bombardment and advanced to attack towards Albaneta and Point 593. The German positions, strengthened and camouflaged over the previous months, had not been subdued by the bombardment and opened a vicious fire, including

cross-fire from Point 575, causing heavy casualties to the 1st Battalion that became pinned on the slopes leading to Albaneta. Tanks attempting to support were knocked out by mines and anti-tank weapons, and the engineers bravely trying to clear paths for them were wiped out by machine-gun fire, 18 of the 20 sappers being killed or wounded. The 2nd Battalion carried Point 593 in its first rush and pushed on towards Point 569, but as the attack faltered due to casualties, including fire from the monastery, the paratroops of 1st and 2nd Battalions of the 3rd Parachute Regiment emerged from their caves on Point 569 to counter-attack. By mid-morning on 12 May they had made six counter-attacks, beaten off by artillery and the Polish troops. The Poles, however, already weakened by heavy casualties, lacked the numbers to withstand the close hand-to-hand fighting, and their survivors fell back. Most of the 2nd Battalion had been killed or wounded.

The 13th and 15th Battalions of the 5th Wilenska Brigade also began their attack towards Colle San Angelo and Point 575 early on 12 May. As soon as they emerged from their forming-up positions, they came under machine-gun and mortar fire which cost the Poles 20 per cent casualties and disorganised the attack. The 13th Battalion, caught in enfilade by automatic fire and with casualties mounting to mines and booby-traps, fell back to Point 706. The 15th Battalion was caught up among thick scrub and thorn, and unsuspected pillboxes built over crevices and cavities in the ground covered by stones and rocks. The Poles could not subdue them, even when other battalions entered the battle, and casualties mounted. On 13 May, with XIII Corps embroiled on the Rapido and in no position to assist, Anders withdrew his shattered battalions to their start lines. The first Polish attack was over. It had failed because of the strength of the German positions, the inability of the artillery and mortars to neutralise them, especially German positions on the reverse slopes and because, like the Indians before them, the Poles did not know the ground well enough. They had also been unlucky. Their attack coincided with a German relief operation, and consequently more German troops and increased firepower were on the positions than normally would have been the case.

Although Anders was ready to renew the attack at once, Leese called a halt. The Poles had, he consoled Anders, drawn the bulk of German fire and reserves away from the XIII Corps bridgehead. Now Anders was to wait until XIII Corps had made sufficient progress in the valley before renewing his attack and effecting a pincer movement with XIII Corps, their attack to be launched when Leese gave the order. In the meantime, they would reorganise, reconnoitre the ground, clear what mines they could, and keep the Germans under artillery and harassing pressure by patrolling. For several more days the Poles endured their existence on the slopes, amid the stench of unburied corpses left from the earlier battles, the rats that fed on them, and the smoke deliberately generated to mask their own positions and supply routes. On the afternoon of 15 May, the Corps was ordered to renew its attack on the morning of 17 May. This time, Anders decided to direct the full weight of the

Opposite page: Troops and tanks of Eighth Army photographed while waiting to advance to cut Highway 6 during 'Diadem', 17 May 1944. The tank is a Sherman, the principal allied medium tank and workhorse of the armoured divisions. In front of the infantrymen stands a Bren light machine gun.

MONTE CASSINO: A POLISH BATTLE

Kresowa Division against Colle San Angelo and Point 575, and the Carpathian Division against Point 593 and Point 569.

In fact, the Kresowa Division's attack began late on 16 May when the 16th Battalion probed through weakened German positions on the slopes leading to Colle San Angelo which, following artillery bombardment, was stormed by the 17th Battalion. They captured most of the feature and held it despite counter-attacks, that died down after 1400. Then, infantry of the 13th, 16th and 17th Battalions went on to take the southern part and the summit. The subsequent Polish report warned future readers that its record of the number of battalions on Colle San Angelo might give an impression of considerable congestion. In fact, it noted, the Polish battalions had been so weakened by heavy casualties that the total number of troops engaged was in reality little more than the equivalent of a single battalion.[11] The Carpathian Division attacked with its 2nd Brigade and tank support. The 6th Battalion attacked Albaneta and by the evening of 17 May was still short of its objective, held by fire from dug-in tank turrets and pillboxes covered with earth and debris, and therefore practically invisible. The 4th Battalion, in a series of attacks and counter-attacks throughout the day, managed to seize and retain a precarious hold on the slopes of Point 593. Casualties were heavy as the Poles, also under fire from Points 575 and 569, came to a halt, exhausted. Anders ordered vigorous patrolling from Point 593. On the morning of 18 May, the 4th Battalion probed forward and captured Point 569, against surprisingly weak opposition. Equally surprising was that no fire had come from the monastery towering above them. Unknown to the Poles, the advance of Eighth Army had prompted Kesselring to order a reluctant Heidrich to abandon the Cassino position. During the night, his paratroops had slipped away along the mountain paths to Villa San Lucia. At midnight on 17 May observers of the British Grenadier Guards in Cassino town were astounded to see German paratroops suddenly emerge from the ruins and run over the slopes of Monte Cassino in short rushes. Artillery fire was called down on them, but most escaped, though troops of the British 4th Division later captured about seventy on Highway 6.[12] At approximately 0800 on 18 May, the 3rd Carpathian Rifle Division ordered its Reconnaissance Regiment, the 12th Podolski Lancers, to send a patrol up from Point 445 to investigate the suspiciously quiet monastery on Monte Cassino.

Opposite page: The battleground: Monte Cassino and the ruins of the monastery photographed after its capture by the Polish Corps. Note the extent to which the buildings withstood heavy air and artillery bombardment.

7
CASSINO AND CONTROVERSY

To the younger generation it is already history, as dead as the soldiers in the cemeteries at the foot of the mountain.

Brigadier E. D. Smith[1]

Battles are fought and soldiers die for reasons that seem obscure or even nonsensical to later generations far removed from the fears and pressures of a war long over. Questions will always be asked about the battles for Cassino in 1944, the most important being whether they needed to be fought at all. The Cassino battles were the consequence of two Allied strategic decisions. The first was the decision to mount an invasion of the Italian mainland with limited forces. The second was the decision to attempt to reach Rome, still with limited forces, once the Allies knew that Hitler had decided that his armies would hold Italy along a defensive line south of the capital.

The Allies fought the first battle of Cassino to assist 'Shingle', itself a dubious concept, attempted with limited forces. It saw Clark's Fifth Army thrown against the Gustav Line, one of the strongest defensive systems in military history, a combination of natural terrain and German military engineering, in an attempt to break into the all-important Liri Valley. Fifth Army attacked in winter, having already exhausted itself fighting through a series of mountain defensive positions, and lacking the strength necessary to break through the Gustav Line. That, of course, is hindsight. At the time there seemed a chance that

Fifth Army and 'Shingle' might succeed, and in war a chance is more than enough reason to send men into battle. The tragedy of the first battle was that the sacrifice at the Gustav Line was in vain. 'Shingle' never got off the beach as intended and it is unlikely, though forever unproved, that even if Lucas had taken the grave risks expected of him that the situation would have changed. For the behaviour of Lucas at Anzio, Clark and Alexander, not Lucas alone, bear responsibility. Clark abetted Lucas in his caution, or was this sound military judgement?

Below: British troops' mopping-up patrol after the capture of Cassino.

Should Alexander have insisted? Perhaps, but Army Group commanders should not be expected to run the battles of their Army commanders, though it is incumbent upon them to ensure that their instructions are absolutely clear, and are obeyed. Alexander appears to have lacked the necessary forcefulness for this, though his task was always complicated by being a coalition commander. Clark, always sensitive as an American commander in what had become a British-dominated theatre, was no easy subordinate. Certainly, had the Germans destroyed VI Corps at Anzio, the consequences for 'Overlord' and Allied credibility with their Russian ally would have been incalculable. As it was, ironically, the consolidated Anzio beachhead compelled Kesselring to stretch his own limited resources, and expend the lives of many of his soldiers in trying to destroy it. This was an important factor in the ultimate success of Alexander's spring offensive.

A further controversy surrounds the first battle, the sacrifice of the 36th (Texas) Division at the Rapido. At the time, however ill-judged and mismanaged the operation, the imperative was to support the beachhead to the north. With Lucas ashore behind the German lines, Fifth Army could not but attack, an imperative reflected by a Congressional Inquiry, demanded by surviving veterans of the 36th Division, that ultimately exonerated Clark of responsibility for the disaster.

The second battle of Cassino grew out of the first, out of the tremendous achievement of the US 34th and 36th Divisions in coming so close to success at Cassino. With the exhausted 34th only a mile from Highway 6 and with a foothold in the town, an attempt to attack with fresh troops seemed more than justified. The problem was that these fresh troops had been held back too long, mainly because of an optimism that II Corps would break through without help, and they had had no time to become familiar with the ground and prepare for their battle. While the arguments of Tuker, and of Juin, who argued for a drive through the mountains instead of the direct attack at Cassino, were sound, they carried great risk. It would have demanded greater confidence in mountain manoeuvre and supply than their experience gave them reason to possess for Alexander and Clark to adopt such a course, and with a time imperative driving them and success at Cassino and Highway 6 and the Liri Valley apparently within reach. The soldiers of 4th Indian Division were not the only victims of the second battle, there was the monastery itself and the monks and civilians within it who died under the Allied bombing. That the monastery would sooner or later be destroyed certainly seems inevitable, but due to factors beyond the control of the soldiers the operation was bungled, and it was the Germans who, ironically, benefited. A reliance upon air and artillery firepower, and the draw of being so near Highway 6 and the Liri Valley, lay behind the third battle, and the hard-fought attempt of New Zealand Corps to take the town. Arguably, with the Anzio beachhead no longer under dire threat, as it was during the second battle, and with Alexander's plan for the spring offensive taking shape, the third battle need not have been fought. That, again, is a hindsight argument and at the time it seemed worth the attempt. It might have succeeded had Freyberg fed in more of his infantry in the early stages of the battle, but there was a view that more troops than could be effectively handled were already in the town and, moreover, Freyberg was not prepared to accept the risk of heavier casualties. Nor was Alexander, and as he proved, nor was he prepared to allow the battle to extend beyond his control when it became clear that Freyberg's opportunity had passed.

'Diadem' provided the advantages previously lacking, sufficient numbers of troops, firepower, air support and improved weather. Then the question becomes whether, in view of the breakthrough achieved at last into the Liri

Below: British troops searching for enemy snipers. Castle Hill can be seen on the right of the picture.

Valley, the Polish Corps attack on Monte Cassino was necessary. It was conceived with the intention of assisting XIII Corps, a reflection of the experience of the earlier battles. It would be very hard to deny that the Polish attack on 12 May, and their consequent sacrifice, assisted the British in the valley by engaging troops and drawing fire that might otherwise have been directed against them. No breakthrough plan could have contemplated leaving the Germans on the dominating Monte Cassino unchallenged. Though it was a tragedy that the Poles were so disadvantaged in their knowledge of the terrain, and that this mistake, that had already cost the Indian Division so dearly, was repeated. The need for the second Polish attack on 17 May is more questionable, but it is also a hindsight argument. It was by no means clear that the Germans would finally abandon their position when they did, and other factors were at work. By then Monte Cassino had become not just a formidable German position but a symbol to both sides. To the Germans, as Heidrich well knew, it represented the courage and superiority of their soldiers defending against Allied *matériel* strength. It boded well for the Atlantic Wall, and German ability to resist future Allied incursions against Hitler's Fortress Europe. The Allies were aware of this, and to them Cassino remained a challenge; the position that had thwarted them so long and cost them so much. The ostensible objective in continuing the attack remained a link-up with the British in the Liri Valley. It also provided the Polish Corps with the opportunity to plant their national flag upon the ruins of one of the most formidable German positions encountered by the Allies during the war. As well as a symbol of Allied triumph, Monte Cassino became a Polish battle honour, reflected in the 3,779 casualties, including over 800 dead, that the fighting in the Cassino sector ultimately cost the Polish Corps.[2] The achievement of the Polish troops was a symbol of hope for their country, a reason that had originally influenced General Anders to take on the battle.

NOTES

Introduction

1. Preface to US Army Training Memorandum No. 3 (March 1944), *Lessons from the Italian Campaign*, PRO WO 204/7564.
2. Janusz Piekalkiewicz, *Cassino: Anatomy of the Battle* (London: Orbis, 1980), pp. 180–1.
3. Admirable studies include W. G. F. Jackson, *The Battle for Italy* (London: Batsford, 1967; New York: Harper and Row, 1967); G. A. Shepperd, *The Italian Campaign 1943–1945: A Political and Military Re-assessment* (London: Arthur Barker, 1968). A more recent work is *Tug of War: The Battle for Italy 1943–45* by Dominick Graham and Shelford Bidwell (London: Hodder and Stoughton, 1986).
4. A most detailed study is the impressive *Cassino: The Hollow Victory* by John Ellis (London: André Deutsch, 1984).

1. The Strategic Imperatives

1. F. H. Hinsley, *British Intelligence in the Second World War*, vol. 3, pt I (London: HMSO 1984), p. 173.
2. Ibid., p. 174.
3. Brigadier C. J. C. Molony, *The Mediterranean and Middle East*, vol. V (London: HMSO 1973), p. 325.
4. Molony, op. cit., p. 194. This figure included nineteen British or British-controlled, four American and four French divisions.
5. Quoted in Sir Winston Churchill, *The Hinge of Fate* (London: Cassell, 1966 edn.), p. 724; Michael Howard, *Grand Strategy*, vol. IV (London: HMSO 1972), p. 433.
6. Churchill, op. cit., pp. 731–2.
7. Joint Intelligence Committee (43) 186 (0) 23 April 1943, PRO CAB 84/6; Hinsley op. cit., pp. 5.
8. The German Armed Forces High Command.
9. Hinsley, op. cit., p. 106.
10. Chiefs of Staff, 24 August 1943, PRO CAB 121/154; Hinsley op. cit., p. 107.
11. Combined Chiefs of Staff Meeting 24 August 1943, PRO CAB 121/154; Hinsley op. cit., p. 107.
12. General Sir Harold Alexander, *Review of the Battle Situation in Italy*, Commanders Conference 1943, PRO WO 193/751.
13. Hinsley, op. cit., p. 106.
14. Ralph S. Mavrogordato, *Hitler's Decision on the Defense of Italy* in Kent Roberts Greenfield (ed.), *Command Decisions*, US Department of the Army (New York: Harcourt, Brace and Company, 1959), p. 237. The Allies refused

to compromise their plans by passing information to the Italians, despite frequent requests for details of the proposed Allied landings and their strength.

15 Mavrogordato, op. cit., p. 238.
16 Mavrogordato, op. cit., p. 239; Kesselring, *The Memoirs of Field-Marshal Kesselring* (London: Purnell, 1974), p. 184.
17 PRO PREMIER 3/124/3 of 10 October 1943. Churchill was attempting to secure Roosevelt's agreement for the employment of a division from Eisenhower's command and sufficient landing-craft to mount an invasion of German-occupied Rhodes, necessary to support operations already embarked upon by the British in the Aegean with limited forces. Hitler's decision to defend south of Rome removed every chance of this.
18 Alexander, op. cit., PRO WO 193/751.
19 Kesselring, op. cit., p. 187.
20 Ibid.
21 Rudolf Böhmler, *Monte Cassino* (London: Cassell, 1964), p. 82.
22 Headquarters US II Corps, Fifth Army, *Tactical Study of the Terrain*, 12 November 1943, PRO WO 204/1096.
23 Ibid.
24 The *Bernhardt Line* was also referred to by the Germans as the *Reinhardt Line*.
25 Martin Blumenson, *Salerno to Cassino* (Washington, DC.: Center of Military History, United States Army, 1993 edn.), pp. 240–2.
26 General Mark Clark, *Calculated Risk* (London: Harrap, 1951), p. 240.

2. Through the Bernhardt Line

1 F. H. Hinsley, *British Intelligence in the Second World War*, vol. 3, Pt I (London: HMSO, 1984), p. 177.
2 Details from Brigadier C. J. C. Molony, *The Mediterranean and Middle East*, vol. V (London: HMSO, 1973), pp. 513–14.
3 W. G. F. Jackson, *Alexander of Tunis as Military Commander* (London: Batsford, 1971), p. 324.
4 Details and Clark quote in Martin Blumenson, *Salerno to Cassino* (Washington, DC: US Army Center of Military History, 1993), pp. 261–2 and pp. 264–5.
5 Dominick Graham and Shelford Bidwell, *Tug of War: The Battle for Italy 1943–45*, (London: Hodder & Stoughton, 1986), p. 135.
6 Sources are Molony, op. cit., p. 592; John Ellis, *Cassino: The Hollow Victory* (London: André Deutsch, 1984), Appendix One, p. 537.
7 Gregory Blaxland, *Alexander's Generals: The Italian Campaign 1944–45* (London: William Kimber, 1979), p.34; John Ellis, *Cassino: The Hollow Victory*, Appendix One (London: André Deutsch, 1984), p. 534.
8 Blaxland, op. cit., p. 34.

9 Molony, op. cit., p. 423 and pp. 602–3.
10 US Army, *Lessons from the Italian Campaign*, APO 534, March 1944, PRO WO 204/7564, p. 5.
11 Molony, op. cit., p. 390.
12 Extract DQMG Letter, 19 February 1944, PRO WO 193/751.
13 Shelford Bidwell, *Gunners at War: A Tactical Study of the Royal Artillery in the Twentieth Century* (London: Arms & Armour Press, 1970), pp. 232–3; Ian V. Hogg, 'The Guns' in *Tanks and Weapons of World War II* (London: Phoebus, 1973); Ian V. Hogg, *British and American Artillery of World War 2* (London: Arms & Armour Press, 1978); *Handbook on the British Army 1943* (London: Arms & Armour Press, 1976).
14 Blumenson, op. cit., p. 262.
15 Blumenson, op. cit, p. 225.
16 Quoted in Ralph Bennett, *Ultra and Mediterranean Strategy 1941–1945* (London: Hamish Hamilton, 1989), p. 255.
17 Fifth Army G-2 Enemy Situation Report, 29 November 1943, PRO WO 204/1096.
18 Source is Molony, op. cit., pp. 515–16.
19 Headquarters US 34th Infantry Division, September 1944, *Lessons Learned in Combat*, PRO WO 204/4635, p.47.
20 See Molony, op. cit., pp. 387–90 for a useful summary of mountain warfare.
21 Rudolf Böhmler, *Monte Cassino* (London: Cassell, 1964), p. 126.
22 US Army, *Lessons from the Italian Campaign*, PRO WO 204/7564, p. 23.
23 Ibid, p. 25.
24 General Frido von Senger und Etterlin, *Neither Fear Nor Hope* (London: Greenhill Books, 1989 edn.), p. 187.
25 Molony, op. cit, pp. 517–19; Blumenson, op. cit., p. 263.
26 US Army, *Lessons from the Italian Campaign*, PRO WO 204/7564, p. 21.
27 Blumenson, op. cit., p. 266.
28 US Army, *Lessons from the Italian Campaign*, PRO WO 204/7564, p. 26.
29 Lieutenant Colonel C. G. Starr, *From Salerno to the Alps: A History of Fifth Army 1943–1945* (Washington, Infantry Journal Press, 1948), pp. 65–6.
30 Source is Blumenson, op. cit., pp. 270–83; Starr, op. cit, p. 69.
31 Blumenson, op. cit., p. 285.

3. The Time Imperative
1 *The Memoirs of Field-Marshal Kesselring*, (London: Purnell edn., 1974), p. 192.
2 Brigadier C. J. C. Molony, *The Mediterranean and Middle East*, vol. V (London: HMSO, 1973), pp. 580–1.
3 General Sir Henry Maitland Wilson replaced General Eisenhower as Supreme Commander Mediterranean, thus the Mediterranean and Italy became very much a 'British' dominated theatre.

4 W. G. F. Jackson, *Alexander of Tunis as Military Commander* (London: Batsford, 1971), pp. 257–8.
5 Martin Blumenson, *General Lucas at Anzio* in Kent Roberts Greenfield (ed.), *Command Decisions* (New York: Harcourt Brace and Company, 1959), p. 250.
6 Quoted in Lieutenant-Colonel C. G. Starr, *Salerno to the Alps: A History of Fifth Army 1943–1945* (Washington, Infantry Journal Press, 1948), p. 84; Ellis, op. cit., p. 37.
7 Quoted in Fred Majdalany, *Cassino: Portrait of a Battle* (London: Longmans, Green and Co, 1957), p. 58.
8 F. H. Hinsley, *British Intelligence in the Second World War*, vol. 3, Pt. 1, Appendix 8 *Intelligence on the German Army's Order of Battle in Italy, January 1944* (London: HMSO, 1984), p. 509.
9 Ralph Bennett, *Ultra and Mediterranean Strategy* (London: Hamish Hamilton, 1989), pp. 261–2.
10 Quoted in Blumenson, *General Lucas at Anzio*, op. cit., p. 255.
11 Quoted in Molony, op. cit., pp. 645–6.
12 Bennett, op. cit., pp. 258–9.
13 Quoted in *Lessons Learned in Combat November 7–8 1942 – September 1944*, Headquarters US 34th Infantry Division, Italy, September 1944, p. 24, PRO WO 204/4635.
14 Figures in Blumenson, *Salerno to Cassino*, op. cit., p. 312.

4. The First Battle of Cassino
1 Martin Blumenson, *Salerno to Cassino* (Washington, DC.: Center of Military History, US Army, 1993 edn., pp. 313–14; Brigadier C. J. C. Molony, *The Mediterranean and Middle East*, vol. V (London: HMSO, 1973), p. 602. These are important sources for the first battle.
2 Orders of Battle in Molony, op.cit., fn. pp. 607 and 608.
3 General von Senger und Etterlin, *Neither Fear Nor Hope* (London: Greenhill Books edn., 1989), p. 190.
4 Held off the coast at Salerno, this proved a shambles due to the inexperience of both naval and ground forces, and the very poor co-ordination between them. General Mark Clark, *Calculated Risk* (London: Harrap, 1951), p. 257.
5 Quoted in Blumenson, op. cit., p. 328.
6 George Aris, *The Fifth British Division 1939 to 1945* (London: 1959), pp. 179–80.
7 Ibid., p. 186.
8 Quoted in John Ellis, *Cassino: The Hollow Victory* (London: André Deutsch, 1984), p. 76.
9 Von Senger, op. cit., p. 192.
10 Blumenson, op. cit., p. 328.
11 Harold L. Bond, *Return To Cassino* (London: Dent, 1964), p. 39.

12 Detailed sources for the Rapido Crossing are Blumenson, op. cit., pp. 322–46; Ellis, op. cit., Chapter V, pp. 90–110.
13 *The Memoirs of Field-Marshal Kesselring*, (London: Purnell Book Services/William Kimber, 1974 edn.), p. 193.
14 Ralph Bennett, *Ultra and Mediterranean Strategy 1941–1945* (London: Hamish Hamilton, 1989), p. 263.
15 Figures from Molony, op. cit., pp. 632–3.
16 Molony, op. cit., p. 633.
17 Ibid, p. 634.
18 Incident related in Molony, op. cit., p. 627, and Ellis, op. cit, pp. 146–7.
19 Messages Alexander to Leese 30 and 31 January 1944, Leese to Alexander, 4 February 1944 in PRO WO 214/29.
20 Source is Molony, op. cit., pp. 700 and 702.
21 Headquarters US 34th Division Report, September 1944, *Lessons Learned in Combat*, PRO WO 204/4635, pp. 1–2.
22 Source is Blumenson, op. cit., p. 303.
23 Quoted in Molony, op. cit., p. 704.
24 Incident related in Fred Majdalany, *Cassino: Portrait of A Battle* (London: Longmans, Green and Co, 1957), p. 87.

5. The Second and Third Battles of Cassino

1 Allied Central Mediterranean Force Appreciation No. 1, *Future Operations in Italy*, 22 February 1944, copy in PRO WO 214/29.
2 Operation instruction quoted in Molony, op. cit., p. 704.
3 F. H. Hinsley, *British Intelligence in the Second World War*, vol. 3, Pt, I (London: HMSO, 1984), p. 190.
4 Ibid., pp. 190–1.
5 Molony, op. cit., fn. pp. 710–11.
6 F. Majdalany, *The Monastery* (London: John Lane/The Bodley Head, 1945), p. 8.
7 Quoted in Raleigh Trevelyan, *Rome '44: The Battle for the Eternal City* (London: Martin Secker and Warburg, 1981), p. 129. Italics in original.
8 Freyberg, letter to Major-General Sir Howard Kippenberger, then Editor-in-Chief New Zealand War Histories, 11 August 1950. Copy appended to *Report on the Events leading to the Bombing of the Abbey of Monte Cassino on 15 February 1944* by Major F. Jones, 14 October 1949, PRO WO 204/12508.
9 General Frido von Senger und Etterlin, *Neither Fear Nor Hope* (London: Greenhill Books, 1989 edn.), p. 202.
10 Major-General F. I. S. Tuker, to Headquarters New Zealand Corps, 12 February 1944, copy in *Report on the Events leading to the Bombing of the Abbey of Monte Cassino on 15 February 1944* by Major F. Jones, 14 October 1949, PRO WO 204/12508.
11 Quoted in ibid., p. 21.

12 The British 12,000-lb 'Blockbuster' bomb was the heaviest blast bomb of the war, intended for the destruction of specific large buildings. A four-engined Lancaster bomber could carry only one, and the weapon was first used in September 1943 by RAF Bomber Command's specialist No. 617 Squadron. Karl Hecks, *Bombing 1939-45* (London: Robert Hale, 1990), p. 168. Tuker was obviously aware of the weapon, but in fact, the scarcity of such specialised bombs meant that they would have been retained by UK-based RAF Bomber Command for its strategic operations. The bombing of the monastery, and of the town of Cassino in March, was carried out by US B-17 Flying Fortress heavy bombers of the US Fifteenth Army Air Force supported by medium bombers – neither attack was an RAF Bomber Command operation.

13 Quoted in *Report on the Events*, p. 9

14 David Hapgood and David Richardson, *Monte Cassino* (London and North Ryde, NSW Australia: Angus & Robertson, 1984), pp. 170–1. This is a detailed published study of the events leading to the bombing of the monastery. Dominick Graham and Shelford Bidwell also provide an important and informative account in *Tug of War*, op. cit., Chap. 12, pp. 191–202.

15 *Report on the Events*, pp. 23–4; Hapgood and Richardson, op. cit., p. 200.

16 Denis Richards and Hilary St. John Saunders, *Royal Air Force 1939–1945*, vol. II, (London: HMSO, 1954), pp. 359–60.

17 Quoted in John Ellis, *Cassino: The Hollow Victory* (London: André Deutsch, 1984), p. 170.

18 Molony, op. cit., p. 720.

19 *Copy of GOC's Report to New Zealand Government on Operations at Cassino*, General Freyberg, Italy, April 1944, PRO WO 204/8294.

20 Sources for the second battle are Molony, op. cit., pp. 710–22; Ellis, op. cit., pp. 174–95; J. F. Cody, *28 (Maori) Battalion* (Wellington: New Zealand Department of Internal Affairs, 1958), pp. 359–62.

21 Allied Central Mediterranean Force Appreciation, *Future Operations in Italy*, 22 February 1944, copy in PRO WO 214/29.

22 Ibid.

23 W. G. F. Jackson, *Alexander of Tunis as Military Commander* (London: Batsford, 1971), p. 276.

24 Details recorded in Molony, op. cit., p. 780.

25 New Zealand Corps, *Historical Notes on the Operation 'Dickens'* (1944), PRO WO 204/8287, p. 4.

26 Böhmler, op. cit., p. 214.

27 *Operations against Cassino by New Zealand Corps* (1944), PRO WO 204/12509, p. 11.

28 Related in Ellis, op. cit., p. 251.

29 Jackson, op. cit, pp. 278–9.

30 Sources for the third battle are Molony, op. cit., pp. 785–801; Freyberg's Report (as note 19); New Zealand Corps' report (as note 27); Historical Notes

on Operation 'Dickens' (note 25).
31 Alexander to Churchill, 20 March 1944, in PRO WO 214/15.
32 *Operations against Cassino by New Zealand Corps* (1944), p. 10
33 Messages 20 March 1944 in PRO WO 214/15.

6. Monte Cassino: a Polish Battle
1 F. Majdalany, *The Monastery*, op. cit., p. 68.
2 F. M. Sallagar, *Operation Strangle (Italy, Spring 1944), A Case Study of Tactical Air Interdiction*, RAND Report R-851-PR (Santa Monica: RAND, Feb 1972), p. vi and pp. 24–32.
3 Martin Blumenson, *Mark Clark* (London: Jonathan Cape, 1985), pp. 200–2.
4 Hinsley, op. cit., pp. 200–1.
5 John Ellis, *Brute Force: Allied Strategy and Tactics in the Second World War* (London: André Deutsch, 1990), p. 325.
6 Gregory Blaxland, *Alexander's Generals* (London: William Kimber, 1979), p. 85.
7 Polish Corps, Eighth Army, 1944 *Operations of 2 Polish Corps against the High Ground Monte Cassino May 1944*, English version, PRO WO 204/8221, p. 44.
8 Böhmler, op. cit., p. 253.
9 Polish Report (as note 7), pp. 11–12.
10 An order of battle is in Molony, op. cit., fn. p. 591.
11 Polish Report (as note 7), p. 40
12 Related in Blaxland, op. cit., p. 101.

7. Cassino and Controversy
1 E. D. Smith, *The Battles for Cassino* (London: Ian Allan/Purnell Books, 1975), p. 9
2 1 Polish Corps, Eighth Army 1944, Operations of 2 Polish Corps against the High Ground Monte Cassino May 1944, English version, PRO WO 204/8221, p. 45.

INDEX

Alexander, General Sir Harold, 9, 15, 17, 19, 21–2, 23, 24, 37, 38, 40, 41, 61, 62, 64, 70, 73, 74, 75, 76, 78, 85, 89, 90, 91, 92, 97, 98, 99, 100, 101, 102, 103, 117, 118, 119
Anders, General, W., 90, 107–10, 113, 115, 120

Baade, Major-General Ernst Günther, 70, 78, 83, 84, 93
Bernhardt Line (Winter Line), 9, 15, 18, 19, 20, 21, 22, 24, 25, 26, 27, 33, 34, 35, 38, 40, 41, 44, 57, 76

British Forces
Eighth Army, 6, 9, 15, 18, 19, 21, 22, 23, 24, 28, 37, 38, 43, 44, 49, 90, 98, 99, 100, 101, 102, 103, 107, 109, 110, 115
X Corps, 20, 21, 23, 24, 27, 32, 35, 44, 49–56, 59, 60, 62–3, 64, 70, 75, 90, 100, 103
XIII Corps, 90, 99, 100, 105, 109, 113, 120
4th Infantry Division, 100, 105, 107, 115
5th Infantry Division, 44, 48, 50–3, 54, 55, 63
46th Infantry Division, 21, 30, 42, 44, 50, 55–6, 63, 64, 100
56th Infantry Division, 21, 24, 30–2, 44, 48, 53–4, 55, 63, 70, 100
78th Infantry Division, 70, 79, 97, 99, 100, 107

Canadian Forces
I Canadian Corps, 90, 100, 107
1st Canadian Infantry Division, 100
5th Canadian Armoured Division, 100
Cassino, 6, 7, 8, 20, 22, 37, 39, 44, 45, 55, 57, 64, 66, 68, 70, 71–3, 75, 76, 77, 78, 79, 80, 84, 85, 88, 89, 90, 91, 92, 93–7, 98, 99, 100, 102, 107, 115, 116, 118, 120

'Castle Hill', 66, 71, 93, 94, 96–7, 99
Churchill, Sir Winston, 11, 12, 13, 15, 38, 39, 40, 61, 89, 90, 97, 98
Clark, General Mark W., 6, 9, 13, 14, 18, 19, 20, 21–2, 23, 24, 33, 34, 38–41, 44, 48, 50, 56, 58, 64, 65, 70, 73, 75, 76, 81, 82, 83, 84, 85, 89, 90, 92, 97, 100, 102, 116, 117, 118
Colle St Angelo, 44, 64, 66, 92, 110, 113, 115
'Diadem', 89–90, 91, 97, 99, 100–2, 103, 108, 119
'Dickens', 91–2, 93–7, 99

Eaker, General Ira, 82, 83, 92
Eisenhower, General Dwight, 11, 12, 13, 14, 15, 19, 38, 81, 90

French Expeditionary Corps
1st Free French Infantry Division, 100
2nd Moroccan Infantry Division, 21, 23, 33, 35, 37, 44, 45–8, 65, 103
3rd Algerian Division, 37, 44, 45–8, 64–6
4th Moroccan Mountain Division, 100, 103
Freyberg, General Bernard, 70, 74, 75, 76, 77, 78, 80, 81–2, 85, 87, 88, 91, 92, 97, 119
Garigliano, River, 17, 18, 20, 32, 44, 49–56, 58, 59, 60, 62, 63, 64, 75, 90, 103

German Forces
Fourteenth Army, 15, 43, 62, 89, 99, 100–1, 103
Tenth Army, 9, 14, 17, 25, 27, 39, 43, 48, 54, 55, 59, 90, 99, 100, 103
I Parachute Corps, 39, 59–60
XIV Panzer Corps, 9, 26, 27, 32, 35, 39, 41, 42, 43, 49, 55, 59, 61, 64, 71, 75, 76, 102, 103, 105
LI Mountain Corps, 102
LXXVI Panzer Corps, 9, 49, 55, 70
1st Parachute Division, 70, 71, 92–3, 99, 102, 107, 108, 110
3rd Panzer Grenadier Division, 33, 55, 62
5th Mountain Division, 28, 35, 45, 48, 49, 55, 102, 110
15th Panzer Grenadier Division, 27, 30, 32, 55, 59, 62, 102, 103, 107
29th Panzer Grenadier Division, 27, 34, 35, 39, 60, 62, 63, 103
44th Infantry Division, 27, 33, 35, 42, 55, 64, 71, 102
71st Infantry Division, 55, 64, 71, 102, 103
90th Panzer Grenadier Division, 39, 60, 62, 70, 71, 93, 103
94th Infantry Division, 27, 49, 51, 54, 55, 59–60, 63, 102, 105
114th Jäger Division, 102, 110
305th Infantry Division, 27, 33, 35, 102
324th Infantry Division, 102
Hermann Goering Panzer Division, 27, 32, 42, 49, 52, 57, 62
Gustav Line, 18, 19, 20, 21, 25, 27, 35, 37, 38, 39, 40, 41, 42, 43, 44, 45, 48, 54, 59, 60, 61, 62, 64, 67, 70, 75, 76, 77, 85, 89, 90, 103, 116, 117

'Hangman's Hill', 67, 92, 93, 95, 96, 97
Harding, General John, 89–90
Heidrich, Major-General Richard, 92–3, 96, 97, 99, 107, 109, 110, 115, 120

Hitler, Adolf, 9, 11, 12, 13, 14, 15, 17, 33, 35, 60, 62, 67, 109, 116, 120
Hitler Line, 18, 107

Indian Forces
4th Indian Division, 70, 74, 76, 78, 79, 80, 81, 83, 84, 88, 91–2, 93, 97, 98, 99, 100, 118, 120
8th Indian Division, 100, 105, 107
10th Indian Division, 100

Juin, General Alphonse, 28, 33, 44, 45, 48, 49, 52, 64, 65, 75, 78–9, 84, 90, 98, 100, 103, 105, 118

Kesselring, Field Marshal Albert, 9, 14–15, 16, 17–18, 22, 25, 26, 27, 28, 33, 35, 37, 39, 49, 54, 55, 56, 59, 60, 61, 62, 65, 67, 70, 75, 76, 80, 84, 85, 89, 90, 91, 99, 100, 102, 115, 118
Keyes, Major General Geoffrey, 20, 34, 42, 44, 50, 58, 64, 68, 69, 74, 75, 90, 100, 105

Leese, General Sir Oliver, 39, 70, 90, 97, 100, 105, 107, 108, 113
Lucas, Major General John, 20, 33, 38–40, 44, 45, 56, 60, 62, 64, 81, 89, 117, 118

Mackensen, General Eberhard von, 15, 62, 77, 85, 89
McCreery, Lieutenant-General Richard, 20, 44, 49, 50, 56, 62, 63, 75, 90, 103
Monastery, 6, 7, 8, 44, 56, 60, 66, 73, 79–82, 83, 84, 86, 87, 91, 94, 97, 98, 103, 109, 113, 115, 118
Monte Belvedere, 45, 64–5
Monte Camino, 20, 27, 30–2
Monte Cassino, 6, 7, 8, 37, 44, 56, 60, 66–8, 71, 73, 76, 79, 80, 81, 82, 83, 84, 85, 86, 88, 91, 92, 93, 94, 98, 99, 103, 104, 107, 108, 109, 110, 115, 120
Monte Castellone, 44, 64, 66, 70, 78, 80, 91, 110
Monte Maggiore, 20, 27, 32–3
Monte Sammucro, 20, 27, 33, 34

New Zealand Forces
New Zealand Corps, 70, 74, 75, 77, 78, 79, 80, 83, 85, 86, 87, 91, 94, 95, 97, 118
2nd New Zealand Division, 70, 79, 86, 93, 97, 100

Polish Forces
II Polish Corps, 6, 90, 100, 107–10, 112, 113, 120
3rd Carpathian Division, 6, 110–15
5th Kresowa Division, 110–15
5th Wilenska Brigade, 110, 113

12th Podolski Lancers Regiment, 6, 110, 115

Rapido, River, 17–18, 22, 44, 50, 56–9, 62, 64, 67, 68, 69, 75, 81, 86, 88, 91, 96, 98, 103, 105, 113, 118
Roosevelt, President Franklin, 11, 13, 15, 38
Ryder, General Charles W., 64, 68

Saint Benedict, 7, 8, 79
San Ambrogio, 50, 55
San Angelo, 45, 55, 56, 57, 91, 105, 107
San Pietro Infine, 33–5, 94
Senger und Etterlin, General Fridolin von, 26, 35, 43, 49, 54–5, 59, 61, 65, 70, 71, 74, 76, 78, 80, 97, 102, 103
'Shingle', 37–41, 56, 58, 60, 61, 62, 64, 89, 103, 116, 117
'Strangle', 99–100

Truscott, General Lucian, 89, 101, 102
Tuker, Major-General Francis, 70, 78, 80–1, 84, 91, 98, 118

United States Forces
Fifth Army, 9, 15, 18, 20, 21, 22, 23, 24, 26, 33, 35, 38–43, 44, 45, 48, 49, 54, 70, 75, 84, 85, 90, 99, 100, 101, 102, 103
XII Air Support Command, 24, 30, 46, 51, 57, 99
II Corps, 20, 21, 24, 27, 32, 33, 42, 44, 50, 65, 66, 68, 70, 73, 74, 75, 76, 78, 80, 85, 86, 90, 105, 118
VI Corps, 20, 21, 22, 27, 33, 35, 37–41, 42, 44, 60, 89, 118
1st Armored Division, 21, 35, 38, 42, 44
1st Special Service Force, 21, 32, 42
3rd Infantry Division, 38, 89
34th Infantry Division, 21, 33, 42, 44, 64, 66, 68–70, 73, 79, 83, 88, 100, 110, 118
36th Infantry Division, 22, 32–3, 34, 35, 42, 44, 56–9, 62, 64, 73, 83, 91, 100, 105, 118
45th Infantry Division, 21, 33, 35
85th Infantry Division, 100, 105
88th Infantry Division, 100, 105

'Ultra', 9, 13, 15, 39, 59, 75, 76–7, 84, 102

Vietinghoff, General Heinrich von, 9, 25, 49, 59, 61, 78, 89, 97, 102, 103

Walker, General Frederick, 32, 33, 56, 57, 58, 62, 81, 91, 105
Wilson, General Sir Henry Maitland, 82, 92, 99